WHAT IS MAN?

IS VOLUME

31

OF THE

Twentieth Century Encyclopedia of Catholicism

UNDER SECTION

III

THE NATURE OF MAN

IT IS ALSO THE

60TH

VOLUME IN ORDER OF PUBLICATION

Edited by HENRI DANIEL-ROPS *of the* Académie Française

WHAT IS MAN?

By RENÉ LE TROQUER, P.S.S.

Translated from the French by ERIC EARNSHAW SMITH

HAWTHORN BOOKS · PUBLISHERS · *New York*

First Edition, February, 1961

NIHIL OBSTAT

Joannes M. T. Barton, S.T.D., L.S.S.

   Censor Deputatus

IMPRIMATUR

E. Morrogh Bernard

   Vicarius Generalis

Westmonasterii, die XXVI NOVEMBRIS MCMLX

CONTENTS

truth. Throughout all our experiences, both intellectual and emotional, we are aware of a deep yearning to transcend the limitations of space and time, to rise above fear and so be at one and at peace with ourselves. It is precisely at this meeting place between our consciousness of our instability and our aspiration towards unity that we are confronted by the mystery of human existence, and find ourselves asking the question: What is man?

This question, when formulated in these terms, involves the whole of man; a fact which certainly both restricts and defines the scope of the answer. It is clear that no single, final answer can be given to a question concerning the ultimate nature of human existence, since it is life itself that furnishes the ultimate and specific answer to the problem of life. Moreover, our question seems to present not so much a problem in biology or psychology as a mystery which we can henceforth describe as "religious", man being an actor in the drama of his own destiny, in the drama of the life which he has to lead.

But the personal nature of the answer surely does not imply that it cannot be illuminated and inspired from within. Because man is a mystery, it does not follow that nothing can be said about human existence, nor that its incomprehensibility precludes all investigation of its structure or all clarification of the meaning of life. Our own opinion is that although in point of fact man, as a unique individual self-conscious subject, cannot be understood by the reason, he can nevertheless be known in those essential structures which constitute his humanity and his human experience.[1] What sort of experience would be that of a subject without a meaning? It is precisely this meaning which is laid bare by reflection when it strives to

---

[1] Here we find ourselves at the heart of contemporary thought, which, in its "existentialist" form, rejects the primacy of knowledge, which it replaces by that of pure experience of the concrete, thereby seeking to explain reality by means of certain emotional trends. Thus we arrive at the conclusion that "existence precedes essence", in the sense that life, to quote J.-P. Sartre, has no *a priori* meaning; it is for each individual to give it a meaning in the process of living.

INTRODUCTION

What is Man? The question, when addressed to each one of us personally, is not the result of mere curiosity aroused by a problem which does not affect our lives; it touches us deeply, because we feel that on the answer to it depends not only the meaning we attach to human life and death, but our capacity for love. In point of fact, it raises the whole problem of human existence. It springs from an awareness of our circumstances and situation which, under the pressure of entirely new situations and events, threatens to overwhelm us with terror, anguish and anxiety.

We live in an unstable world, stamped nevertheless with the deepening imprint of man's human nature. Behind the imposing achievements of science and technology looms the threat of war and civil strife, in which man's desire for victory brings about his own ruin. Man towers in astonishing dominion over the visible world, whose most hidden sources of energy he is able to tap; but he knows that all the time he is in danger of allowing himself to be mastered and crushed by the very forces he had thought to control. This is the paradox of the human situation, which as soon as we become aware of it, brings us face to face with the enigma of being itself. Our consciousness is weak, our desires inconstant. We eagerly seek to take possession of persons and things, but the realization of our hopes often leaves us unsatisfied. We are the slaves of our emotions, and strangely infirm of purpose. Finally, death, the universal and ineluctable end for which the intellect can find no remedy, seems to crown the inherent contradictions of our life. Is life then, my life, worth living? And yet, in spite of the perplexities, the disappointments and tribulations to which we are subject, we long—dimly, no doubt, but genuinely—to know the unravel the intelligible structures of the human mystery. This reflection appears to be essential if we wish to make sense of our existence as we experience it, and so be able ourselves to be the mainspring of a human life more rich in human values. The present study therefore aims to elucidate the meaning of "man" by bringing his structures and his concrete conditions to light.

We may call this reflection "Christian anthropology", thereby indicating the specific object of this book. By "anthropology" we mean reflection on the structure of man as he fulfils his destiny through a series of voluntary and temporal acts, always within the perspective of the Christian revelation. Our first task is to make clear what this perspective is, as a preliminary to bringing forward certain major themes.

We begin by saying that revelation is not a branch of anthropology, nor does it ever provide us with a treatise on man. Its specific purpose is to reveal to us God's historical plan, its aim is to make us sharers in the life of God himself. It is essentially the doctrine of salvation for man, and it is so in the most absolute form salvation has taken—the incarnation of the Word of God who came to accomplish that divine plan which was inaugurated by the adoption of a privileged creature and re-established by the redemption of that same creature, and will be consummated by the universal judgement at the end of time. It is clear that this scheme provides both the framework and the impetus for any attempt at a Christian anthropology, since it sets man in the sole context of God's plan, of God's will and of the incarnation of his Son. In other words, from the anthropological point of view, revelation determines the principal themes, thereby furnishing the faith which seeks to understand the realities that are revealed to it with an inexhaustible treasury of truth; and revelation not only fixes the limits of this treasury, it does more, for it is the force at work within it. From another aspect it may be said that the anthropological consideration of man can root faith in an understanding more ready to receive it.

An anthropology may be termed Christian not only in virtue

of its connection with revelation, but also because it takes its place in a tradition of investigation and study stretching back through medieval philosophy to the writings of the Fathers. Limitations of space prevent our tracing all the links in this historical chain. We must content ourselves with isolating constant factors which may serve as landmarks to guide us on our way.

When St Augustine, in the *City of God*, writes, "Man is a wonderful thing, because God made him in his own image, yet he remains a mystery to himself" he is expressing the fundamental view of man held by the Fathers, particularly by Origen, St Athanasius and St Gregory of Nyssa. The basis of their whole anthropology was derived from the words of Genesis, "God said, Let us make man, wearing our own image and likeness": as Gregory of Nyssa says, "All is summed up in the story of creation, which tells us that man was made in the image of God." This theme, which not only demonstrates the dignity of man, but comprises all his prerogatives, provided the Fathers with a basis for exploring man, analysing his psychology and demonstrating incontrovertibly that man is truly man only when he transcends himself and returns to the God in whose image he is made. The laws of the spiritual life are deduced by the Fathers not empirically but from the very structure of the soul, which is conceived as created in the image of God from whom it derives its basic vital energy. It should be noted that this theme of the image, which stresses the importance of man and his invulnerability in respect of his relation to God, came to be one of the dominant themes of Christian thinking about man: it occupies the most prominent place in the thought of St Augustine, and was taken up and developed by St Thomas Aquinas, particularly in the passages of the *Summa Theologica* dealing with the creation of man. And this theme of the image, which the Greek Fathers employed to lay bare the mystery of man, enabled them to reveal to us a new dimension of man which seemed to them to be absolutely essential: namely, the basic unity of all men. Nor did this new dimension seem to differ from that in which the very dignity of man consists, since the divine image is the same image in all men. "The whole of human nature," says Gregory of Nyssa, "from the first man to the last is but one image of him who is."[2] The conviction of the Greek Fathers, a conviction which had to meet the pagan philosophers' mockery of this claim to unity, was that man as an individual person and man as a species are not in opposition but contribute each to the making of the other, since all men are made in the unique image of God. Thus the patristic tradition offers us two major constants, which it will be our business to examine: man created in God's image, and the unity of all men.

We have already pointed out that St Augustine also makes these themes his own and places them at the centre of anthropology. Thus, in his treatise *On the Trinity*, because he believes that man was created in the image and likeness of God, he claims to recognize in the spiritual activity of the human soul not merely a trace, but far more, an image of the Trinity; whence he proceeds to an analysis of the intellect, the will, and the memory. He is increasingly imbued with the idea that the personal and the universal life are of necessity on an equal footing. The reverse of a systematist, he throws a revealing light on the basic features of man in his concrete condition, in his quest for happiness. He makes us aware of our shortcomings, thereby inducing in us a salutary concern and directing us towards God, who is able to enlarge our awareness. In reading him we cannot fail to become aware of mankind's advance towards unity and of the very concrete sense of man's pilgrimage towards beatitude.

The central problem dominating Thomist anthropology is that of the unity of man, a problem which was bound to confront earlier Christian philosophy, since the Gospel is concerned with the salvation not only of the soul but of the entire

[2] Quoted by H. de Lubac, S.J., in *Catholicisme* (Paris, 1947), p. 7; Eng. trans. by Lancelot C. Sheppard, *Catholicism*, London, Burns Oates, and New York, Longmans, 1950, p. 5.

man. St Thomas' solution to the problem, which we shall meet later, is a simultaneous demonstration of the mystery and the sacred and inviolable character of man: for man is a mystery, in that he consists of both matter and spirit; and he is sacred, in that existence can impinge on him only through his soul.

Image of God; oneness of mankind; concrete nature of existence; unity of man, consisting of body and soul: these are the constant factors in the Christian tradition which will guide us in our inquiry, the fundamental theme of which is God's revealed plan which will be accomplished by the gathering together of all things in Christ.

With these considerations in view, we shall devote the first part of this book to an attempt to lay bare the springs of human action by explaining the basic structure of human personality underlying the mysterious and paradoxical complexity of the union of body and soul in man. In our second part we shall consider man in his concrete historical situation, in his reality as a fallen and redeemed being.

PART I

"GOD CREATED MAN IN HIS IMAGE"

THE BASIC STRUCTURE OF MAN

CHAPTER I

"THE FIRST ADAM"

The starting-point for Christian thought on man has always been the first chapters of Genesis, as we have stressed in our outline of the invariable factors in a Christian anthropology. It is in these chapters that the earliest thinkers found the stimulus for their reflection.

From a literary point of view, the language in which these chapters tell the story of the creation of the universe and of man is full of artless and popular imagery. We are not dealing with a didactic treatise, and it would be useless to attempt to include these accounts in our modern classification of the sciences of man. Genesis offers us the essential impetus for reflection. It provides the jumping-off ground for the exploration of human nature, which is nothing less than the revealed plan of divine love: God's purpose in creating man was none other than to raise him to the supernatural state, in which his whole being, the body included, would one day be transfigured in the personal enjoyment of supreme happiness.

By returning to Genesis we enter the long tradition of Christian thought on man and, in a sense, provide the mind with the light of a knowledge which will enable it to penetrate the mystery of the human fact at every level.

THE COMPOSITE NATURE OF MAN

"And now, from the clay of the ground, the Lord God formed man, breathed into his nostrils the breath of life, and made of man a living person" (Gen. 2. 7).

These words reveal God's twofold operation, the creation of

the body and the creation of the soul. They show us man as composed of a body, taken from the earth of which it is therefore a part, and of a "breath", the Hebrew word employed signifying both respiration and soul, the principle of life. It is by the union of these two principles that man becomes a living person, that is a creature entirely animated by a principle which links him to the nature of God. We are presented with a single living creature harmoniously uniting in itself a body and a soul, the body yielding complete obedience to its soul, the soul yielding complete obedience to its God, with the result that we have the hierarchical and harmonious integrity of a creature entirely new and entirely submissive to its creator. This is the prime characteristic of the mystery of man, who is revealed as the frontier between the two worlds of body and of mind which are combined in the ontological unity of his personality.

It should be noted that, strictly speaking, this account of the creation of man neither affirms nor denies the hypothesis of an intermediate stage in which the human body might have been formed at a lower level of life; nor does it assert or deny the gradual evolution of matter to a point of perfection at which the organism became fit to house a rational soul. What the Catholic creed in fact insists upon is the special intervention of God in the creation of man; and it is an article of faith that the creation of the human soul at least was the immediate act of God.

This harmonious unity, in which a soul created directly by God assumed matter into itself, did not exempt man from the duty of a spiritual self-discipline which gives free play to the powers of the soul, as appears from the story of the temptation and of the injunctions of God relating to the "tree of life". From the moment of his creation man clearly appears as a being who is the frontier of two worlds to both of which he belongs. He is a creature of time and eternity, he exists both in the world and, by virtue of his possession of a soul, transcends it. The suffering caused by man's awareness of his composite nature and its limitations and which, after the fall, was to lead to shame and revolt, lay dormant previously precisely because of man's intimacy with God, who is the centre of gravity of existence and the principle of human stability and rectitude.

Here then is our first important line of thought: human nature is composite, a union of body and soul.

IN THE IMAGE OF GOD

Man, a composite creature belonging to the two worlds of matter and spirit, was created in the image of God. It is at this point that revelation affords us the clearest insight into the inner reality of man and, at the same time, bids us to have that boundless respect for our nature which prevents man from allowing himself to sink to the level of an object, for he is a spirit and consequently the true image of God. We begin to see the sacred character of this being, who is created—and here lies the mystery—to live with God. Man was sacred from the fact of his creation: he becomes pre-eminently sacred through the religious nature of his loving relationship with his God. "And God said, Let us make man, wearing our own image and likeness" (Gen. 1. 26).

The words "wearing . . . our likeness" exclude the notion of equality. But this verse proclaims a similarity of nature between God and man, so that we can say that just as God is mind and will, so too is man. Hence we may draw the conclusion, which later we shall be in a position to amplify, that man is a person, that as a spirit he is in a fundamental relationship with God, and that this relationship constitutes the crux of his mystery. This is not, of course, to define the mystery, but it does provide us with a hint that greater value attaches to man than an empirical view might lead us to believe. From the very first entrance and the first steps of man in history Revelation leads us towards this mystery of man, a mystery which is clearly and above all religious, since man is spiritually linked to his creator. By the words "made in God's image" we are to understand that man is endowed, by the express will of his creator, with a vital principle of a spiritual order. From this he derives both his stability and his intelligibility, while at the same time he remains unfathomable to his fellow men.

In this way, we are shown the superiority of the vital principle in Adam over the vital principle inhering in other creatures, and man's position in and transcendence of the universe. "Let us," continues the story in Genesis, "put him in command of the fishes in the sea, and all that flies through the air, and the cattle, and the whole earth, and all the creeping things that move on earth." Man is therefore in an order apart, superior to all the living creatures around him, and consequently the centre of the realm of values and ends. Indeed, situated as he is between creatures which are purely material and those who are purely spiritual, he welds them into a wholly new creation. He is the meeting-point, the fusion into one nature, of the visible world of the body and the invisible world of the spiritual soul. It is through him that, in a sense, the visible universe finds its meaning and takes its place in the hierarchy of beings which form the universe of God's creation. According to revelation, man is clearly the centre of this creation: he is the microcosm placed at the uppermost limit of the visible world to be its citizen and its priest. In the words of St Gregory Nazianzen: "God builds the palace and then instals the king within it."

Here we have a second line of thought. Man was created by God to be an image of him, and he becomes thenceforth a person living in harmony with himself, exercising spiritual dominion over the universe which was created for him, and for whose upward movement he assumes the responsibility, for it is through him that the universe fulfils itself and plays its part in the triumphant hymn of the mystery of creation.

VOCATION

Behind the story of Genesis we discern a deeper relationship, rooted in the similarity between man and God, in whose image he was created. This relationship is one of vocation, by which is understood man's living response to the call of his creator's love. And love's rhythm is one of call and response. On the one hand God freely calls, on the other is the response man has to make in a history which constitutes his destiny. These facts reveal the fullness and spiritual reality of personality. It is at this point that we embark on a scrutiny of the main characteristics of human nature as exemplified by its response to the uncreated love of God.

God's purpose in creating man was to admit him to intimacy with his creator and to assign to him the rôle of carrying out in history the divine plan. It is for this reason that Adam is described as "the type of him who was to come", that is Christ who was to be perfect man. (Rom. 5. 14). It follows that man's relation to God is twofold. It is not only that relation which, in consequence of God's creative act, enables man to take his place in the realm of existence, it is also that living relation with God, based on man's spiritual nature as God's image, which, in his capacity of incarnate spirit, he has to live out in time. Indeed, since he is an image of God, made in his likeness, man has to "bear this likeness" in his everyday life. This is man's vocation which, beginning as no more than a promise, fulfils itself in the progress of a spirit that grows ever more aware of itself and more deeply responsive to the call of the divine love which impels it forward.

It follows that man, into whose being this vocation is written, moves towards an ever closer likeness to God in whose image he is made. In the words of Origen: "It is man's duty to achieve this likeness by striving to imitate God so that, having originally acquired, through being honoured by his creation in God's image, the possibility of attaining perfection, he may finally achieve a perfect likeness by performing his allotted tasks." The innermost being of man, from which his capacity for action springs, seems therefore to consist in this living relation to God. This relation is both a call and a response; it enlists man's vital powers by making it possible for him to achieve the fundamental purposes of his being.

This prospect is familiar to all who have contemplated the mystery of man. Sartre himself, though obviously drawing diametrically opposite conclusions, went so far as to write:

> Whatever myths and rites may then be found in the religion we are considering, God is first of all apprehended by the "heart" of man, as the being who proclaims man's existence and defines him in relation to his ultimate and fundamental project. . . . God, the supreme value and end in the transcendental order, represents the permanent and ultimate limit of being in terms of which man insists upon being told what he himself is. To be a man, is to move towards the attainment of the existence of God. Or, in other words, man is fundamentally a desire to be God.[1]

Called to this union with his creator, it is man's duty, at the first moment of his conscious life, to accept freely the gift which is made to him. This acceptance is a prerequisite of the religious bond, which is the distinguishing mark of genuine existence and consists in a personal response to the divine initiative. Because he was created in the image of God, man's deepest longing is to fulfil himself in love's consummation which is unity. But this fulfilment must be preceded by putting love to the proof. Gift and movement of acceptance must be reciprocal. At this level is seen both the nobility of man and the dramatic and paradoxical nature of human existence. For man, though he exists, has to become what he is by his own efforts through the flux of time and the contradictions inherent in his status of a being composed of both matter and spirit. Man has to become of his own free will what God intends and bids him to be.

Thus we see our first parents, undergoing their vocation as an active and painful experience of God's gift, since they are to pass that test which is the distinguishing mark of the human personality and consists in the free effort made by the creature in his movement towards his creator. In this upward struggle of mankind the love of man for God could only be a free act, or

1 *L'Etre et le Néant* (Paris 1948) pp. 653–4.

rather the free acceptance of the free invitation of God. It should be observed that in creating man in his own image and likeness, God accepted the risk involved in his plan for the divinization of his creature, and that there is an indissoluble connection between the ontological dignity of grace and moral danger. Indeed, if spiritual blessedness, the object and goal of man's existence and the fulfilment of all his ends, consists in the intimate sharing of God's love, it follows that, in the creature, that love can consist only in the free union between man's will and God's will, and can operate only in the form of that obedience which is the religious expression of the living relationship between man and God, as can be clearly seen from the story of the temptation and fall (Gen. 3. 5–22). Hence the necessity of a period of trial, since for a person obedience means submission to something which both transcends and fulfils him: it is the natural condition and privilege of any creature made in the image of God, and characterizes the vulnerability of his freedom.

These considerations illustrate the dramatic nature of human existence, which always runs the risk of repudiating the end for which it was created and the basis of its dignity by refusing to follow its vocation and respond to the appeal of love.

These preliminary positions with which revelation confronts the believer are mysterious in character. We need hardly say that we do not intend thereby to imply that the spirit should remain passive in the presence of an overwhelming reality: what we have in mind is rather a profoundly reverent investigation of a "sacred" reality, for, if man is a mystery, it may perhaps be because the mind first sees him as possessing a fullness of being which we may grasp yet never exhaust. It sends us back to a deeper reality for it is of the nature of mystery that it does not destroy intelligibility; it is its foundation.

Man is a mysterious being because he combines in himself the two apparently heterogeneous worlds of flesh and spirit, the temporal and the eternal, and because his condition makes him simultaneously "immergent and emergent". There must needs be mystery in the case of life, which is a total living unity not reducible to the categories of thought. If we bear in mind the well-known saying of Pascal that "man infinitely transcends man" we arrive at the heart of the mystery: man is invited by grace to enter the realm of God's love, a realm inaccessible to our unaided reason. The final mystery resides in man's likeness to God, which is the source of his vocation and the *raison d'être* of his being; it gives him his active rôle within the orbit of God's plan.

The mystery of man, as it has been revealed, is a region of light into which we must enter by the door of reflection. Such an investigation is indeed necessary if we are to root our faith in man as created in the image of God in an understanding which is all the more ready to accept in that it is actively aware of this mystery and has to unravel its deep complexities. Our reflection will then lead us to discovery, to a deeper knowledge, and so take its place in the tradition of Christian anthropology.

CHAPTER II

MAN IS BODY AND SOUL

"The human soul is a kind of horizon and frontier between the corporeal world and the incorporeal world."

(St Thomas, *Summa contra Gentiles*. II, 68)

THE PROBLEM

Man, created in the image of God, is a being at the frontier, both in his body and his soul. He is the meeting-point between the visible world of the body and the invisible world of the spiritual soul. He stands on the summit where the world of matter meets the world of the spirit; he stands too on the horizon between time and eternity. We are struck by the paradoxical nature of this limited being, the plaything of contrary forces: matter and spirit, extension and thought, time and eternity, the individual and the universal. We perceive that, before becoming the expression of a psychological drama, this ambiguity is fundamental to the complex structure of the human being, for feelings derive their depth from the reality out of which they spring. A cursory glance at the whole of our experience, whether of ourselves or of our relations with the outside world, makes us conscious of this dual allegiance.

By our possession of a body we find ourselves subject to the laws of space and time, of motion and duration, and included in a physical universe governed by determinism. We are a part of this universe in which we are situated and which is the orbit of our existence. We are one unit in a whole, and probably neither the strongest nor, materially speaking, the wealthiest. This circumstance leads to a realization of the frailty of our being which, because of the sheer burden of its body, tends to dissolve in cosmic or social multiplicity. Sometimes we experience the desperate anguish of being submerged in "the infinite immensity of space of which we know nothing and which knows nothing of us".

But we are spirit and so can escape from matter, space and time. We have the capacity to rise above limitations and despair. We are capable of understanding, and in the act of understanding we can extricate ourselves from material conditions. We can bring the presence of the mind into the midst of reality. "If the universe were to crush him, man would still be more noble than that which killed him, because he knows that he dies and the advantage which the universe has over him; the universe knows nothing of this. All our dignity consists, then, in thought."[1]

There are certain crucial questions which inevitably arise, and given the fact that the mind seeks totality and unity in the multiplicity of phenomena, they are the crux of all reflection on the nature of man. Is it one and the same being in his entirety, who is both body and mind? And what kind of a unity is achieved? Doubtless we feel that this is no mere academic question since, as we shall have occasion to show, on our understanding of this unity largely depend our way of life, our conception of death, and our view of social relations. The question lies at the very heart of all anthropology, which is bound to account for the unity of man, both body and soul. Should either of these elements usurp a privileged status, man tends to disintegrate both as a person and as an agent. The recovery of man's fundamental unity appears to be absolutely necessary, if we are to avoid the twofold temptation of monism, a permanent temptation for the human mind which always finds it easier to reduce the problem to a simple question of black or white rather than admit its complexity: on the one hand "spiritual-

[1] Pascal, *Pensées*, Everyman Edition, p. 97.

ism",[2] with its conception of the body as an impediment or prison; on the other hand "materialism", which considers man as one element among many, without access to eternity because he is strictly bound up with space and time. In short, this exclusive alternative of spiritual or material man deprives him of his humanity: either he disintegrates or he is alienated from the world which is his proper home. In the words of Kierkegaard, we must avoid "the madness of those who think the world is a dream, and the madness of those who think the human soul is an empty word".[3]

It is a far cry from this antinomy to Christian thought through which runs this assertion of the unity of man through the union of body and soul. For Christianity is not primarily a doctrine of immortality and of the soul's destiny: its essential teaching is the salvation of the whole man, not solely the liberation and purification of the soul. The remote ancestor of the latter is no doubt Platonism, and a more recent forebear is the dualism of Descartes; but the Church has always refused to accept as her own doctrine of man the view that presents it as a disciplining of the body designed to free the soul from all ties of the flesh.[4] In fact, Christ came to redeem all things, thus accomplishing the hidden purpose of the Father "to resume everything in him, all that is in heaven, all that is on earth" (Ephes. 1. 10). It was not the soul that Christ came to save by the offering of his body: "in accordance with this divine will we have been sanctified by an offering made once for all, the body of Jesus Christ" (Hebr. 10. 10), it was man in his concrete

[2] This term is used here, obviously enough, in a philosophical sense and has no reference to what is called "Spiritualism" in ordinary usage. Any such confusion is out of the question in French which renders the common meaning of the word by *le spiritisme—Trans.* See footnote 3.

[3] "Spiritualism" and "materialism" are here employed as general terms indicating an attitude of mind rather than a system of philosophy, and expressing the almost permanent opposition in the history of thought between empiricism and idealism.

[4] This was the attitude taken up by the Church in the fourth century against the Montanist, Gnostic and Manichean heresies. In 1311–12 the Council of Vienna defined as of faith the union of the soul and the body.

unity of soul and body. Proof of this statement may be found in the pages of 1 Corinthians dealing with the resurrection: "If what we preach about Christ, then, is that he rose from the dead, how is it that some of you say the dead do not rise again? . . . This corruptible nature of ours must be clothed with incorruptible life, this mortal nature with immortality" (1 Cor. 15. 12, 53).

The whole problem, then, is to understand the human composite, to distinguish the elements composing it, and to apprehend it as a living whole forming a genuine unity. Our whole effort of thought will enable us to account for the unity of man, and by a process of uniting without confusing, and discriminating without separating, we shall grasp the truly original and irreplaceable quality of his life as a person. At the outset, two conditions appear absolutely necessary: in the first place, the soul and the body must be distinct though not heterogeneous; in the second, the two must constitute a strictly unified being, whose ontological nature in all its fullness it will be our task to describe.

REALITY OF THE SOUL

Man, because he was created in the image of God, is spirit. This, as we are told in Genesis, is the most salient characteristic of his nature. It is this that allows him to take his appropriate place in the universe in the hierarchy of created things, and to progress beyond the threshold of animal nature. But in order to grasp the nature of a living reality we must fathom its proper mode of operation, which always brings us back to being, since action is the epiphany or manifestation of the being who acts and finds himself involved in his action. This is the course we propose to adopt in order to discover what the soul really is. Our task, in other words, is to become aware of our thought so that we may then return to the field of our existence, whose profound originality we shall determine, thereby achieving a knowledge of that "me" which both underlies and transcends all our descriptions and all our bodily activities. We have to reach the central reality within us, we have to make effective the "presence of mind" within us in the very act itself of the mind, and although such contemplation may appear to remove us from earthly reality and the drama of our existence, it serves in fact to lead us back to earth bringing with us a light which should make it possible for us to see more clearly the unity of man in the union of body and soul.

All the philosophies have taught that the life of the intellect is one of the principal characteristics of human existence, since it is knowledge that enables man to become aware of what he is, and so to see himself and to be seen by others as man. We shall consider intellection from the point of view of its own dynamic force, that is, as opening the way to, making us present to, leading us into, the self. By this means we shall be in a position to uncover the reality of the being from whom it springs.

It is undeniable that "the object all the processes of cognition continually have in view is that which is, reality as it is and whatever it is, including all its aspects, all its potentialities and implications: not only the reality which I am, but the reality which I am not, the me as well as the not-me." Granted this primary aim, we can perceive that the specific good towards which intelligence moves is being, that intelligence is at rock bottom a readiness to make contact with being which it consequently seeks to appropriate. Intelligence, in fact, strives to obtain a truer and more faithful idea of what is. It seeks a clearer understanding of reality, to lay bare its pattern of relations, its whys and wherefores, with the ultimate object of reaching the unity which underlies and envelops diversity: herein resides the meaning of all scientific activity at whatever level. It therefore seems that intelligence, in pursuit of this aim, must transcend the phenomena of space and time. For beneath the particular, and the specific here and now, intelligence discovers the universal, the principle of unification, and expresses it in the form of a personal judgement. Finally, since this readiness to make contact is essentially equivalent to the unravelling of the meaning of the real, it provides an illustration of the free expansion of thought in its search for the intelligible.

From this readiness to make contact with the whole of reality, which is the basic characteristic of the mind, a number of consequences may be immediately drawn. If it is to have any scope, it means in the first place that the being who is its subject is able to distinguish the self from the non-self. In fact, to be ready to make contact is to be able to encounter and to welcome. Before we can welcome anything we must first withdraw into ourselves: that is, we must simultaneously possess ourselves and distinguish ourselves from that towards which we are moving, and this leads us back to a certain state of inwardness which must be an awareness of and a presence to the self. It is precisely this which testifies to the immaterial nature of the mind. Ready as he is to make contact, the knowing subject is not enclosed within himself, since he is capable of possessing being and of summing it up in himself in all its universality. Yet this capacity is linked to a deliverance from everything material, to the mind's situation beyond space and time. Matter, indeed, makes the subject one particular fragment of a species, one part of the universe; it cuts him off from all else. Since he is thus subjected to the conditions of space and time, he has a fixed abode and hence is unable to rise to what is universal, to sum up reality in himself. Therefore this readiness to make contact with reality is a sure sign of the *immaterial nature* of the knowing subject. More than this, it is an "intention", by which we mean that it is no mere attitude of waiting for other realities to come but a light or an illuminative power in the intelligence capable of providing the object in view with an intelligible content, with the result that the concrete percept is stripped of its individual characteristics and so makes it possible for the mind to reach the universal. According to St Thomas Aquinas, this illuminative power which comes into operation only through active contact with the universe, the orbit of our existence, is like a reflection in us of the divine intelligence. Once more we return to the theme of creation in the image of God.

The activation of our readiness to make contact, which aims at the true understanding of reality, can only lead to a vital identity of subject and object, and knowledge is achieved by the realization of this synthesis of the knower and the known, this most intimate union of the Ego with the Other. This presence is a process of appropriation, it has nothing in common with physical assimilation but refers us back to a spiritual reality. In fact, a living creature who assimilates food assimilates it into himself and causes it to disappear; whereas knowledge is a process of mutual assimilation and interpenetration in which subject and object retain their original identities. In other words, the art of knowing differs from physical assimilation in being an act of spiritual communion. Hence this deepest and most intimate of unions is justly termed a mutual presence, since knower and known do not give rise to a third term; the subject does not become like the object he knows, he actually is the object. Thus we see how the act of knowing is the expression of existence at its highest and most significant level. Nothing in life is more truly alive or more authentic, since the union achieved is the closest possible, and takes place on the plane of spiritual existence, the realm in which alone there can be a mutual presence.

This consideration brings us at once to the true nature of the thinking creature. In so far as he thinks, he must be spiritual, since the type of presence which is a living experience in his act of knowing is essentially spiritual; knower and known become one, while each remains itself as far as its own natural existence is concerned.

The fact that we are capable of contact with the totality of being, that we are able to reach it beyond its spatial and temporal aspects, and identify ourselves with it in a living relationship, not only reveals an immaterial and spiritual principle, but also necessitates, at the very source of this intellectual activity, an actual concrete subject, a reality which exists in the spiritual order, since there is a necessary correspondence between the mode of action and the mode of being. It is, in fact, by reflection that we discover ourselves as existing subjects and in our highest mode of being, that of the spirit. We experience ourselves as inward, as the source of our intellectual acts; we realize experimentally that we are "mind" present *within* and through all the activities in which we engage. This existence within oneself, unlike that of matter whose every part is external to every other part, is the privilege of the spirit, which is the subject of existence. To be within oneself, to be present to oneself therefore necessarily implies a spiritually subsisting subject which is the source of all our intellectual acts, and for that very reason manifests itself as always present and disclosing itself everywhere.

The spiritual stability of the soul's existence and its independence in relation to matter, time and space are therefore the consequence of its infinite plasticity, which enables it to apprehend the whole of reality, and of its inwardness, which enables it to be present to itself and is the sign of the fullness of its existence.

This consideration makes it at once possible to assert the immortality of the soul. Since in its act, as we have seen, the soul is able to embrace all reality by its presence to and its communion with it, since too the soul exists within itself, we have deduced that it is a subsistent, immaterial, spiritual reality. In other words, we have understood that it is a spirit situated beyond space and time, essentially independent of change, and transcending the body. The soul is therefore naturally immune from corruptibility and there is nothing within that can cause its disintegration; in other words it is immortal. A being, in fact, is perishable and therefore mortal in so far as it is subject to change and involved in space and time by reason of its material nature. It is true that in the concrete the soul, as we shall shortly emphasize, can only operate with the help of the body. But we must note that this relationship applies only to the activity, not to the nature of the soul, which as such has no need of a body, being self-sufficient. It follows that nothing can derogate from its integrity, and that the destruction of the body cannot involve the destruction of the soul, which continues to exist after the dissolution of the partnership between the two.

From the psychological point of view we are made aware of the immortality of the soul through that desire to live for ever which is thoroughly characteristic of the consciousness of each one of us and is found at the centre of all our acts and thoughts. This longing never to die is not an empty dream, and in expressing it we are stating a truth which, although we may not recognize its profundity, draws its value from the very depths of our being. The wish not to die, but to transcend space and time, seems to us to be the psychological manifestation of the ontological stability of the soul, that is, of its spiritual and immortal existence: it would be worthless, were it not based on the actual structure of the mind. Thus we become aware that our existence has deeper roots than our empirical existence, and our existence as beings in this world, since its very principle is spiritual and immortal. This certainty of the reality of the soul in all its dimensions will therefore determine our attitude to a world in which we find ourselves, but which cannot enclose us because, as far as the inner nature of our being is concerned, we transcend it.

THE UNITY OF SOUL AND BODY

We have just said that the human soul is a spiritual and immortal reality. To this we must add that the soul is capable of being united to a body. The capacity for association with a body is natural to it, not only because it may be united to a body *per accidens*, but because this union is essential to, and characteristic of, the nature of the soul, which, as St Thomas says, "is by its nature adapted for union with a body". The human soul differs from an angelic spirit in being an incarnate spirit united with a body, situated in space and time, and needing a body in order to pursue its activities, to enter the realm of thought and so attain its final perfection and realize its vocation. Therefore, owing precisely to this essential capacity for association, the union of soul and body is never to be regarded as a fall or punishment. The body is not the prison of the soul but an instrument placed by God at the service of the soul, for the latter's fulfilment; far from being a punishment this union becomes a salutary bond. Furthermore, in the light of revelation we need only refer to the story in Genesis and to the mystery of the Incarnation, for it was a complete human nature that Christ assumed in his divine personality, a theme which we shall meet again in the dogma of the resurrection of the body at the Last Judgement.

This union of soul and body is experienced by us in all our conscious activities, and our experience tells us that their subject is ourselves and not part of ourselves. The body is the sole vehicle of both thought and love. Hence, when absorbed in these activities, we are aware, no doubt in a very general way, that it engages the whole of our personality, our feelings, our intellect and our will, which knows and loves. Further, in all our actions, in so far as they express ourselves to ourselves or to others, there are two dimensions, one corporeal, the other spiritual, from whose union these actions derive their meaning. From the circumstances that our concrete actions take place in time and space they are transitory and material events; but at the same time the spirit is present at the centre of these actions, and were this not the case they would be devoid of all meaning. It is strictly true that the value of a human act, which as such takes place in a historical context, depends on its bond with the spirit, with the spirit as incarnate, which communicates to it all its own human fullness and unitive power.

Consequently, whether I consider my act at its source or as a fact, I shall always find in it these two dimensions and their unity; time and eternity, matter and spirit, body and soul. The

pairs of terms seem indeed to provide the texture of all our
thoughts and actions. Yet in spite of the undoubted legitimacy
of this conclusion, the problem still remains how to account for
the way in which these two realities, body and soul, are so
united as to be the foundation of man's being. How is any
union possible between the body which is located in space and
time, subject to flux and change, and materially determined,
and the soul which is beyond space and time, spiritual and
immortal, the principle of presence and fullness of being?
What is the nature of their union?

From the outset it seems that we must reject the theory
according to which man is a mixture of the spiritual and corporeal substances which constitute his being. It is indeed
immediately obvious that, before such an arrangement is
possible, the components as such must disappear, failing which
the result would be not an arrangement but chaos. Now St
Thomas points out that the soul is immaterial and consequently incorruptible, and cannot therefore form a compound
with the body. If it did, its own nature would disappear. At the
opposite extreme of the theory which fuses the soul with the
body to the extent of destroying the nature of the former, we
find Plato making so sharp a distinction between soul and body
as to leave them with no more than an external connection; a
view which reappears in part in the philosophy of Descartes.
This amounts to asserting that man's nature is only in his soul,
which uses a body as an instrument: how then can we account
for the intimate union of body and soul which we experience in
every act we perform? Further, we may draw attention to the
fact that a great number of processes, such as the operations of
the senses, are carried out by the soul in conjunction with the
body. By this very circumstance we are surely led to the conclusion that man is not simply a soul making use of its body, but a
genuine whole compounded of soul and body. This consideration in turn leads us to ask whether the union of soul and
body may not be the union of two realities of which the one,

while retaining its identity, perfects the other, that is animates
(informs) and develops it, and is, with and in the other, situated
in time and space.

When we asked ourselves what activity appeared most
specifically characteristic of human nature, we answered that it
was thought; through it man transcends the universe in which
he is placed and rises above his animal nature. Subsequently we
were led to see the principle of this activity as spirit, that is as
inwardness, a spiritual and immaterial presence, and consequently as act and perfection. But we added that the human
soul requires a body to enable this act of human thought to be
carried out, lacking as it is, not in intelligence but in sense
operations to bind it to the world of matter. It is indeed by the
body that man's soul is subject to the laws of matter, that is to
space, time and motion which are the expression of change and
imperfection. We now visualize the union of the body and the
soul as a relation uniting what is act and perfection, by virtue
of being spirit, to what is potency and imperfection by virtue of
being matter, or in scholastic terms as the union of matter and
form.[5] From this point of view it follows that the soul, the
principle of spiritual presence and therefore of actuality, is the
"act" of the body, that is the principle which informs the body,
makes it real, enables it to play its part and causes it to be.
From this "act" man receives all that is positive in his being:
the soul as "act" is sufficient to establish man in his specific
being, by causing his body to be and by endowing it with life,
sensitivity and understanding.

But in order to understand the unity of man we must go
further and place ourselves within the order of existence. As a
matter of fact, what exists is not a body and a soul but a man.
We exist by one and the same activity. If the spiritual soul is the
form of the human substance, and if man is a unity, and not
two natures existing side by side, the reason is that this form

---

[5] These terms are borrowed from Aristotle's philosophy. Matter
(potency) is the passive principle which receives being and activity. Form
(act) is the active principle which bestows being and activity.

implies of itself a relation to existence, and must be understood
as the reality which makes possible man's existence as man. In
short, the unity of the subject is impossible unless it is founded
in existence. To be precise, we have seen the soul as a subsisting
reality, that is a reality which exists within itself, implying that
property which makes of it an "in itself" as it faces existence;
it is therefore able to make its own the act of existence for
which it is created. Man is composed of body and soul, whose
relation is that of determined and determinable, perfect and
imperfect, immutable and mutable: he owes it to the soul alone
that he is a subject, centred on himself and possessing his own
incommunicable existence. In fact, the soul as a subsistent
reality is that by which existence endues the whole man with all
that he is, sensibility and intellect, that by which his body maintains itself in existence. Man therefore maintains himself in the
unity of his being, soul and body, only because his subsistence
is that of the spiritual soul, which enables him to possess his
existence and consequently to make it issue in action. Thus the
unity of man is not a unity of two conjoined elements, but the
unity of his act of existing which comes to him through his soul.

For any consideration of the nature of man, the consequences of this ontological unity are wellnigh inexhaustible:
they will crop up constantly throughout this book. Nevertheless, we are already in a position to grasp the fact that man is
mysterious and, so to speak, "sacred". The mysterious character of this being, who is a unity of spirit and matter, is exactly
defined by the words of St Thomas Aquinas which we have
placed at the head of this chapter: "The human soul is a kind
of horizon and frontier between the corporeal world and the
incorporeal world." The fact that man, in his specific nature,
maintains himself in existence only by virtue of the subsistence
of the spiritual soul imparted to the human composite, whereby he is enabled to possess and perfect himself in freedom,
reveals to us the paradox of his greatness and of his weakness.
In so far as he is a spirit activating a body, man remains subject

to material conditions; his unity is precarious and needs to be achieved from day to day. In so far as he is a spirit which transcends the body, he participates in the realm of the spirit and is in relation with God and the eternal: he is in time, but is already in eternity.

Because of the sacred and inviolable character of his existence, man is the noblest and most perfect thing in nature, since his existence comes to him through his spirit alone, while his body has no existence in act other than that which it shares with his soul. Consequently, man exists not only as in himself and by himself, but even more as *for* himself, that is as a person, and personality expresses being at its fullest, and existence in its most integrated form. We shall deal with this consequence in a later chapter: for the moment we are concerned with the light thrown on the value of the body by this vision of man's unity.

THE VALUE OF THE BODY

Man's existential unity clearly reveals the significance and nobility of the body. We can envisage the body only against the background of the soul and in its relation to the spirit, from which, by sharing its existence, the body derives all its nobility. Consequently, in speaking of the body we are speaking of that "companion" of the soul without which the soul could neither fulfil itself nor give itself in knowledge and love; the union between the two is so close and vital that after the separation brought by death, the soul, as it were, awaits the Last Judgement when it will rejoin its companion and share its own glory with the body. St Thomas observes that the soul's bliss will then overflow onto the body so that it also may enjoy the soul's state of perfection. For this reason St Augustine says that God made the soul of so powerful a nature that, out of the fullness of its bliss, a mighty stream of incorruption flows into lower nature. We shall reveal the body's nobility which is based, as we know, on spiritual existence, if we inquire how it makes this spiritual presence possible, and how it enables the soul to fulfil itself.

The most fundamental characteristic of spirit is *presence*, which on the human plane operates in constant reciprocity with the body. "The inner man is sustained solely by the outer man, the outer man solely by the strength of the inner man:" there can be no realism without a "principle of exteriorization", nor at one and the same time without a "principle of interiorization" (E. Mounier).[6] We shall therefore show how the body enables us to be mentally present to ourselves, to the world and to others.

G. Madinier has rightly said, "Existence has to be won; it is a presence both active and effective; the body is the instrument of this presence, which is presence to the self because it is presence to the universe". This is because man's primary awareness is of the concrete created order in which he is included through his body. It is through and in this reality that we first experience our existence, that is, our presence in the world and the presence of the world in us; the emergence of self-consciousness requires the impact of the external world, but we apprehend this world in the first place through our body, which appears to be the point at which consciousness of the world and of self will begin. The child, while still an infant, is entirely subject to his "organo-affective" occupations, consisting of alternate sleeping and waking, the rhythm of breathing, vague gesticulations which have no purpose as far as the world outside him is concerned and indicate a state of initial lack of differentiation between subject and object. Nevertheless, step by step the child will become conscious of his body through the differentiation of his motor activities and through the operation of his senses, which, as they are awakened, seem daily to enlarge his space and to locate him more and more within it. Exploration of his body reveals to him that it is his own. Sight and hearing gradually differentiate him from his surroundings. We are well aware of the way in which self-consciousness is increased during infancy and childhood by the handling of objects and the mastering of the physical world through action

[6] *Qu'est-ce que le Personnalisme ?* pp. 68–89.

and play. The soul has been defined as a spirit which acquires its consciousness of self as it builds up its body by relating it to the world. Our presence to the world by means of our body is a factor of our presence to ourselves and a guarantee of the forward movement of our thought, because in this relation, which must never be abandoned if we are to be sure that our knowledge will deepen, we are undergoing that experience of "the same" and of "the other" which constitutes consciousness and, by the same token, our insight into all reality: for we are "the same" because we exist, and we are "other" because we exist in a different way. Finally, this experience shows us that the world is neither a vague unity nor yet an aggregate of separate units. This fact undoubtedly opens a gateway, which it is the business of education to widen, into the life of the spirit and into that presence of the spirit which is the sign of personality and signifies both inwardness—consciousness of the self—and outwardness—presence to the world.

Our presence to the world, the sphere of our existence, before being a mental presence is to begin with a physical presence, and the one conditions the other. Through our bodies we are located in space and time, in an environment, that is in a network of relations, and consequently of discriminations or connections, according to circumstances. This situation makes us part of that universe, a unique point included in that immense network of cosmic forces and movement. As such, we are subject to the cosmic laws, we are no more than a fragile unity which tends by its own weight to relapse into multiplicity. Yet man, who is at the same time both spirit and matter, "lives" this situation, this physical presence to the world. Hence man, passing beyond the level of absorption in the universe, inseparable from bodily existence, will become present by his spirit to this universe, and in order to do so, will use the body as an instrument.

By our insertion, through our bodies, into space and time, we become historical beings, since man's historicity springs from his "fleshly" presence to the world by which he belongs to a

race, a people, a country and an epoch. Hence we are able to
write the story of our salvation, giving to time, to which we are
united by our body, a direction and significance through our
spiritual presence. It is through this spatial and temporal situation that we are enabled to bring about our own progress and
the upward movement of the universe, by establishing in it that
spiritual presence which converts a simple process of "becoming" into a history by giving it a meaning and purpose—to
promote the advent of the spirit. "Time is both the condition of
our life and the sign of its inadequacy. It is in time that our
life's growth proceeds between the two boundaries of birth and
death; it is in time that every act of knowledge and of will is
accomplished; without time we should be inert and reduced to
the status of a thing; it is through time that we exercise our
initiative and share in the work of creation."[7] For man, to
share in the work of creation is, to a large extent, though
doubtless this is not his only or most essential contribution, to
set his mark on all things through his labour. In fact revelation
teaches us that man was made head of the whole of God's
creation and was placed by God in the "garden of delight" to
cultivate and tend it (Gen. 2. 15). God entrusted his creation to
man in order that he might humanize and complete it by making it share in what man is. Man, by his labour, projects around
himself a human and spiritual environment, by stamping the
world with the seal of his spirit, which is the image of God. In
performing this task man both fulfils and frees himself. But this
result is brought about only by means of the body, the instrument whereby the human spirit is incarnated in the whole
creation. That the body is the instrument of our history is
shown not only by the fact that it is through it that we are
present to the world and subject to the process of becoming,
but also because it is through the body that we have to stamp
the mark of our spirit upon the world, for the body, in its union
with the soul, is the instrument of the soul's presence and
activity. It is by means of the body that eternity is "sown" in
the soil of time, which then becomes history. Finally, it is once

[7] L. Lavelle, *Le Moi et son Destin*, Paris, 1936, p. 220.

more from revelation that we know that it was through the body that God entered into human history through the mystery of the incarnation of his Son.

The body, which is the instrument of the presence of spirit to the self and to the world, is also the instrument of our presence to what is other than ourselves. There seem to be two characteristic features of this presence, it is an inner experience and an outward expression, by which we mean that the spirit moves in both an inner and an outer direction and the body plays its part in this movement.

To begin with, in intellectual activity the body is the instrument of spiritual presence, in that without its help no cognitive acts can take place. It is by means of my body that I apprehend reality. My consciousness is in the world through and by means of an organized body, and in my act of knowing I look at the world with everything that I am, both intelligence and senses, and I apprehend intelligible reality by throwing light on the datum perceived. This explains the discursive aspect of our cognitive acts and their multiplicity, but at the same time it implies that none of these acts can claim priority, since it is the whole man who knows and, as we shall see later, looks at reality in its totality. Hence, knowledge comes through various mediating agencies, one of which is sense activity: hence we can say that the body is made to serve the act of thinking, that is the act of spiritual presence which is knowledge. It is not an intellect that thinks, it is the whole man, that is an intellect served by a sensibility and a sensibility penetrated by intelligence. Through the union of these two functions in his cognitive act man is able to experience concrete reality in an experience which is neither purely intellectual nor purely sensitive, but human, that is, both. This experience, in fact, can be neither purely sensitive, since if we confined ourselves to sight we should never know what we are seeing, nor purely intellectual, since to intelligence there corresponds an idea which, being abstract, has no existence outside ourselves. It follows that the intellect lives, in its own mode, the reality which it understands; but this is only possible because the body supplies the intellect with the conditions necessary for the realization of its act, for the presence in it of the object.

The body is present not only in the act of understanding but also in the act of the will, which is love. Love undoubtedly sets out from the inner realm of the spirit to reach the beloved object at its point of highest value, that of the spirit; and the goal of its journey is a superior mode of existence, since the lover strives for the closest possible union with the beloved. But human love is necessarily subject to the conditions of our incarnate being; it cannot dispense with the body. It is through the body that we live our love, and the denial of the body reduces our life to a rigid pharisaism whose features are no longer human. It is through the gestures of the body in all their manifold forms that we are able to express our love to the beloved, and these gestures, indispensable to every human lover, become the real signs of our affection. But we must go even further, for the body is not merely the instrument whereby our affection is made tangible. It can become, by a new manner of approach leading to the depths of man's unity, the organ of love in an act whereby the spiritual person gives himself immediately and unconditionally through the gift of his body. This is wedded love, a fleshly act performed for the sake of a spiritual act, in which "I" and "You" become "We" in the most intimate communion of all, involving as it does the whole person both body and soul in one act. It is no doubt true that the part played in this act by the body can degrade and materialize love, even to the point of rendering spirit itself carnal; and we shall see that this risk is very real in fallen man, whose enfeebled spirit no longer guarantees sufficient mastery over the flesh. Nevertheless it remains true that genuine wedded love is spiritual. Established by two persons to form their unity in body and spirit, it requires them to behave towards each other as persons, incapable as such of being loved except for themselves. Hence we can begin to see that the physical realization of such a communion can develop the life of the persons who live by it and spiritualize the body itself, which is at the service of a union which increases its own dignity.

Since our presence to what is other than ourselves, achieved as it is through the medium of the body in the act of knowing and willing, is inward in character, it is also, by the same process, an outward *expression*. As the human person is incarnate, it cannot become present to the beloved except by a physical manifestation in which the body is a sign, that is the vehicle of a reality deeper than itself which it is its duty to reveal. The sign is in reality no more than the manifestation of the spirit by means of the body or, in the words of J. Mouroux, "the body expresses the soul", revealing the spirit in all its mystery. Man's gift of himself has always this character of a sign, since it springs from his being, which is the union of soul and body.

The human body, as revealing his spirit, is the means whereby man gives and expresses himself to others. This revelation takes place at different levels. We have seen how in wedded love the whole body can become the true and living sign of one person's gift of himself to another, to the extent that the two persons "become one flesh". All love seems to imply this gift of our spirit through our body. It is the love of God that moves man in his unity: man's response is not abstract, but expressed in words that are a prayer, or in concrete communal activity, in the liturgy, where everything—chants, attitudes, rites—combine to give expression to the inner realm of the soul. This response is also manifested in the gesture which makes me present to the poor, the outcast and the suffering, a gesture that gives expression to my love for God: "For I was hungry, and you gave me food, thirsty, and you gave me drink . . ." (Matt. 25. 34). But on a deeper level man responds to God by the gift of his whole being, body and soul, and that is why, when God takes possession of him, he can become a witness, one who by word and deed makes God present in the midst of men: hence the profound remark of Bergson: "The mystics have only to exist. Their existence is a rallying cry." Through his body man becomes the sign of God in space and time. Finally, the body is the greatest gift of the love of God, who gives himself and expresses himself in his incarnation.

It is also through his body that man becomes able to communicate with the spiritual reality represented by signs. While
expressing our thoughts by signs, we at the same time make our
own thoughts of others through signs, which thus form a link
between two minds which, by means of them, are able to share
the same feelings and the same inner life. We are well aware
how, in the field of art, the training of the body, which sharpens
its senses, when combined with an education of the soul, is
indispensable for the comprehension of the mystery revealed by
the artist, once the opacity of matter has been overcome by the
spirit. It is then the whole man, body and soul, who communes
with the work of art, and the feeling that grips him is both of
the senses and of the spirit. As further evidence of the part
played by the body in its appropriation of the sign as the source
of communion, we may take the extreme case of those who
have been rightly called "souls in prison", those, that is, who
have been blind and deaf and dumb from birth or almost so,
and hence before their education could begin.[8] In these cases
the awakening of the intelligence has proved possible, and has
been accomplished solely by means of the language of the
hands, by the discovery of the meaningful relation between a
gesture and some desired object. Furthermore, it is noteworthy
that in the case of normal children who have the use of all their
senses, the whole task of the teacher consists in arousing in the

[8] Cf. Louis Arnould's *Les âmes en prison* which gives an account of the
case of Marie Heurtin. The nun who was nursing her, noticing her attachment to a penknife belonging to her, took it away from her. The sick girl
was angry and so the sister gave her back the knife, but at the same time
she arranged the child's hands so that one cut across the other. After
several attempts, once the sick child had grasped the idea that she was to
repeat for herself the movement that had been suggested to her, she was
allowed to keep the knife. The experiment was repeated with other objects.
Gradually the child acquired the habit of making gestures to indicate anything she wanted. She was soon able to use the Braille alphabet, and there
was no longer any idea beyond the reach of her mind. We see that the
"cornerstone" of all this training was the sign.

English readers should know Helen Keller's *The Story of my Life* and the
incident of the water which, in her case, was the delivering and revealing
sign.—*Trans*.

mind, by successive approximations, the consciousness and recognition of signs; a process that cannot be carried out without the co-operation of a body on the alert, since a sign is no more than a gesture or movement of the body, indicating something other than itself and the intention of the person who makes the gesture or movement.

The body derives its nobility from the existence communicated to it by the soul, and its dignity from the fact that it is, within the unity of the personality, an instrument and a companion. But it is obvious that this union of body and soul is not something achieved once and for all, a fact which reveals in man, body and soul, a certain ambiguity rooted in his very nature. That man consists of body and spirit means that these two realities are made one for the other but each preserves its own character. In this union the soul does not become the body nor the body the soul. The body, while made to be actuated by a soul and so to be its servant in order that the soul may be itself, remains nevertheless in the order of matter, and therefore in that of change and decay. This being so, it is clear that the body, though the instrument and companion of the soul and its efficient helper, at the same time hinders and resists the soul and restricts its development, since it is always through and by means of the body that we approach and express reality, and are present to ourselves. It is, in fact, through his body that man is rooted in an animal nature, by which we mean that he is the sport of unconscious forces and hidden energies which reveal themselves at every level of human existence and affect the soul in its function of quickener of the body. Here we enter the realm of the instincts and drives which form the temperament. It will be sufficient here to note briefly a few facts that will adequately reveal the concrete condition of man in his unity.

Within this complex two principles may be distinguished. To the ancients they were known as the "concupiscible" and the "irascible" principles, one concerned with what will preserve the nature of being, the other with destroying anything which may be opposed to it. More specifically, we have on the one hand sexuality, which aims to unite creatures for the purposes of creative fecundity, on the other hand aggressiveness, which urges the ego to assert itself before and against others. We note also that these two appetites or forces overlap and interpenetrate. To begin with they are completely non-moral, they are neither good nor bad. Freedom from these tendencies is incompatible with being a man. It follows that the Stoic ideal, magnificent though it may be, is inhuman; for it is no disease in the soul to be joined to a body and to be affected by its variable behaviour. The soul, therefore, under the influence of these tendencies experiences feelings of pleasure or of pain. These are affective phenomena and may consist of emotion, which accompanied as it is by complex physiological phenomena weakens the coherence of the mind and our adjustment to reality, and passion which, unless controlled by reason, becomes a blind impulse overthrowing the balance of psychological life.

Thus the body is both an asset and an obstacle to the soul, with which it is linked in the closest, existential union. There is no reason to be scandalized by this fact. On the contrary, we should accept the reality of the whole man, in its darkness and its light, but at a deeper level, in its unity. This acceptance brings us into contact with life, since it leads us to recognize that the union of body and soul is a unity of tension and opposition which, although potentially a source of conflict, invites man to master his body and make it his perfect and faithful servant. We have already remarked in connection with man's original state of harmony, that the latter demands effort. We can now see that the fundamental requirement for the union of soul and body is man's duty to become himself by acquiring the mastery over his body. In other words, his task is to become more and more the image of God, to be increasingly obedient to his creator, and so a body ever more submissive to his soul. His task is to become a person, and the conception of personality leads to a new and deeper insight into the essential structure of man.

CHAPTER III

MAN IS A PERSON

"A person means that which is most perfect in nature."
(Summa Theol. Ia., Qu. 29, art. 3)

Through the new insight afforded us we perceive that in calling man, in the unity of his body and soul, a person, we reach the most profound reality in man's mystery, when he is considered as a spiritual individual and a subject essentially open to God. The revelation of the mystery of man, that he was created in the image of God, thus receives a readier welcome in our mind. Man, like all his fellow creatures, exists in space and time, as part of the universe which contains him. But his peculiar attribute is that spiritual dignity which places him at the frontier of two worlds, because he exists by reason of his subsisting spirit; it is through the latter's subsistence that his whole being is flooded with existence. Revelation, as we have already stressed, has taught us that the creation of man in God's image is not merely a question of the resemblance to God shared by all creatures as a result of their existence. Man's special resemblance to God derives from the fact that God is a spirit and man proceeds from him since he possesses a spiritual soul as the principle of his life and his unity.

Recognition of personality is not a definition of it, since man, the image of God, carries within him an inexhaustible mystery. Nevertheless the conception is illuminating since it throws light on his complex originality, and reveals the dynamic force which is proper to him.

We shall discuss personality under its two complementary aspects of structure and evolution.

THE STRUCTURE OF THE PERSON

We must observe at the outset—and this observation is fully valid in the context of contemporary philosophy—that there can be no question at this level of reflection of describing our subjectivity as such, that is, of explaining our personality and our interior life in conceptual terms. It is obvious that subjectivity, the inner life of the ego, is something secret, which means that it is even to some extent obscure to itself. *A fortiori*, since it is interior life, it eludes the observation of other people. It can be said that subjectivity, as such, cannot be conceptualized, it cannot be known by means of concepts, because all reality, when known in this way, is objectified; and objectivization will always give a false account of subjectivity, the inmost nature of our own or another's personality. But in respect of its essential structure, personality is not falsely represented when it is made an object, because personality possesses a nature which makes it what it is, and by which it is the subject exceeding in depth the whole universe of objects.

As Maritain has very rightly pointed out, the best way of discovering the structure of the person would seem to be to consider the relation between personality and love. True love is an approach of spirit to spirit; in other words, it bursts forth from one person and reaches another. It does not stop short at possession but moves towards being at its deepest and most secret. This centre calls love to itself and to it love makes its way, for it can give and give itself, it can receive the other as a person. But to be able to give ourselves we must first exist in the highest possible way, we must possess and master ourselves, since the gift of love is the gift of what is most invulnerable in man; hence freedom is involved.

Self-possession and self-mastery mean that we maintain our *unity*, and this is one of the first characteristics of human personality. By unity we mean not the psychological unity which consists in awareness as opposed to inadvertence or diversion, indispensable though such awareness may be, but the ontological unity of an existing being. Unity is the expression of stability, the self being indivisible but owing its existence to its separation from other things. This is what is meant when we say that a being which is one is a being which exists *by* itself, in that it possesses its being, and *in* itself, in that it is self-sufficient. But unity of this kind is common to all concrete individual beings: it is not an adequate foundation for the gift of self, because a being which is merely *in* itself and *by* itself is bound up with matter and lacking in that degree of autonomy which would enable it to give itself without losing itself. We must make the transition to the spiritual order, and speak of spiritual unity; for self-possession and self-surrender are properties of the spirit which is capable, by very reason of its immateriality, of being present simultaneously to itself and to others. Personality is rooted in the spirit in so far as spirit maintains itself in existence and is capable of a superabundance of it, and personality is nothing other than the subsistence of a spiritual soul communicated to the human composite. Hence the spiritual unity which characterizes personality is the expression of the greatest possible fullness of existence: or (to quote again from Lavelle) "the essence of being at its most profound, that is, the fact that being *is* by its very *act*".

Personality, because it is spiritual unity, signifies that one is within oneself, it signifies an act of presence to oneself. It is an inward, clear presence to oneself, and its act of presence is an act of presence of the spirit. This inward presence is the very basis of self-mastery and of freedom. Personality, being in fact presence to oneself, has the power of freely perfecting itself by itself determining the ends it shall pursue, and of freely giving itself to such an extent that the essence of personality coincides with the essence of freedom. We therefore say that the person is *for* itself, thereby expressing its absolute and unique character in the universe. It constitutes a universe in itself, a microcosm of greater excellence than the entire material universe: for man, because he is a person, is the image of God.

Whereas material being forms part of a whole to which it cannot open itself, the person, precisely because he is spiritual unity and inward presence, is by definition, an *open* being. In the person the most spiritual inwardness coincides with the greatest degree of outward movement in every direction: his slightest act leads him deeper into himself but only by giving him a more universal character. Here we approach what might be called the dynamics of the person: the more interior it becomes the more open it is, the greater its ability to accept, and at the same time to offer itself. By knowledge and love, in fact, the person is able to place itself on a level with all things. Through intellect and will it can communicate to others everything that it is without loss of self, and can receive all that they are without causing them to lose it, since this interchange operates on the spiritual plane and is therefore authentic, for the person finds itself again in those to whom it gives itself. To its spiritual nature it owes its essential capacity to receive and to give, to turn inwards and to leap outwards, to communicate and to be present. Because of its inwardness it brings about that unity which is the consummation of the destiny of all mankind.

Since his unity consists in the subsistence of a spiritual soul imparted to the human composite, man is truly a person; that is, he realizes in his being that spiritual unity, the inwardness and "openness" which are the characteristics of personality. Within the sphere of our immediate experience he is the supreme and absolute value, in the sense that the human person, if it is to maintain its integrity, cannot under any pretext be treated as an object or as a means. Nevertheless, man is very far from being purely and simply a person. His personality is that of a material individual, forming part of the world of space and time and forced to exist in part on infra-personal planes which make it vulnerable and easily influenced; it is the personality of person incarnate, and hence is situated at the lowest level of personality. This circumstance reveals the basic complexity of the structure of man, who is simultaneously an individual and a person, or in more concrete terms, outside and inside time, of the flesh and of the spirit. *Qua* individual, since individuality is based on matter and implies situation in space, man is a part of the universe in which he lives and, as we pointed out above, he is subject to the laws of matter which, by its very nature, tends to relapse into multiplicity. Individuality and personality are the two poles of human nature. They indicate both its fullness and its limitations. Two facts become immediately obvious. They are implicit in any case in our consideration of the union of body and soul. In the first place, individuality and personality are not two separate realities. Since man exists only by reason of the subsistence of his spiritual soul he is wholly individual by virtue of what he derives from matter, and wholly personal by virtue of what he derives from spirit.[1] In the second place individuality is not to be considered as something evil, since it is the concrete condition of our existence. What is bad is to give the primacy to the individual aspect. If it is to be authentic, the progress of man should be in the direction of personality: it should involve, within the unity of being, a diminution in the importance of individuality resulting in an enhancement of the importance of personality and its dynamic force as the principle of inner unity and man's "openness" to others.

This observation leads to a further consideration to which we shall have to return later. Human personality is an incomplete and unstable reality. Its incompleteness is due to the fact that it is not absolute spirit since its being and its existence are not perfectly identical, nor is it presence pure and simple. It follows that such a spirit strives *proprio motu* to be one with itself, or more accurately with its own centre, which is its relationship to God, so that this relationship may become more

---

[1] This comparison, borrowed from J. Maritain, may help us to understand the unity of man. We are simultaneously individuals and persons, in exactly the same way as a picture is wholly a physico-chemical compound by virtue of the pigment of which it is composed, and wholly a work of beauty by virtue of the painter's art.

vital and unifying. The human person strives therefore to complete and fulfil itself. In the often quoted words of Pindar, a person has to make itself what it is; it has to become, and this becoming constitutes all its greatness, so that it may be said that to be a human person is to be called to self-transcendence. Human personality has to bring into effect that spiritual unity which, to begin with, is a promise of what is to come, by increasing the mind's mastery over the body, by converting the body into the privileged instrument whereby personality rises to a higher degree of spiritual being, and by making it more responsive to the activity of the spirit. In other words the human person has to win its personality.

But the human person, while called upon to transcend itself, remains fragile, vulnerable and complex: only by the most painful effort can it struggle towards that super-being whose call it hears within itself. It cannot escape the tension between the two poles of its being: its vocation is to achieve its own unity, yet it suffers the pull of disintegrating forces. If it follows the bent of its individuality it runs the ever present risk of deterioration and dissolution. In short the achievement of personality, which is obviously its ultimate goal, is accomplished in an atmosphere of struggle and tension. It is in the midst of this conflict, characteristic of his instability, that man succeeds in becoming a person, in so far as the life of the spirit dominates and assumes into itself the life of the flesh.

Thus we see that the essential characteristics of the structure of the person are spiritual unity, inwardness and "openness". At the same time, it is incomplete and unstable. But we must go further still, for the human person is only relatively independent *qua* person: we must add a further characteristic; it is also a centre of relationships.

The human person is fundamentally a relationship with God, who is the original and abiding source of its existence. Hence this relationship constitutes the being of the person, which has no existence other than that imparted to it by God. Here we reach the very root and dynamic principle of personality, an absolutely privileged relationship providing us with a still deeper insight into the ontological reality of creation in the image of God. Indeed God, the cause of the existence of all creatures, is in touch with man not through his body but through his spirit, through whose subsistence existence comes to him. It follows that this privileged relationship is most appropriately called spiritual, and it is in this sense that man is truly "the image of God". And far more, this relationship also implies presence. For since to exist is the most central and the most intrinsic characteristic of all creatures, it follows that God, as the cause of their state of existence, is in all things by that most intimate presence which defines the degree of their being, and his presence is the most intimate because it is that of the most absolute transcendence. "God," says St Thomas, "by the excellence of his nature transcends all creatures and is nevertheless in them all" (*Summa Theol.*, Ia, Qu. 8, art. 1, ad 1m). Consequently, since existence reaches us through the soul, the spiritual principle, we see that this presence is a living presence, or rather a living relationship, since it brings the created spirit into contact with the divine spirit.

For the human person, then, this relationship constitutes a summons, and it is at this point that we draw near to the very life of the person both in its origin and its final destiny. Its origin, for God, by creating us in his likeness as spirits, and as spirits necessarily incomplete, creates us as a call to others to be in communion with us, since the impulse to enter into communion is an intrinsic characteristic of the spirit. Its final destiny, since this communion aims at union with God, and the person strives after a progressively more active resemblance to God, whose image it is. We should note that this tension does not imply a wish to become God, which is impossible and would destroy all living relationship, but to live in union with him. Thus the human person is evidently made to be a call to communion because God wills that we should attain personality, or again it is made to be our own vocation. Here we arrive at the purpose behind the dynamic quality of the person which, although it has to work to become itself and under perilous conditions, is not the author of the direction its life is to take, since in its very being it is summoned by God, and this reveals a radical and inescapable direction. This problem will shortly appear again when we come to consider the question of freedom.

We have said that the most spiritual inwardness coincides with the greatest degree of outward movement in every direction, by which we mean that the person, although independent, is not for that reason a closed entity, but desires to enter into communication. Hence we are led to see the human person in the last analysis as a relationship with human beings. It is the whole man who is in relationship with the world of men, and so we shall here find again, in an intimate connection, the two poles of his being, his individuality and his personality. This has led J. Mouroux to say that the human person is at one and the same time a member and yet the whole; he is a point on the circumference and yet the centre. In these two terms "member" and "the whole" we are given the two modes of the human person's union with the world of men, or with human society.

As a member, the human person is considered as one who shares the human nature which is in fact present in every human individual. Accordingly it is a part of that great whole which includes it and for which it was created. It is a member of a body to which it subordinates itself and in which it has a specific function to fulfil, and its own good is inferior to the good of this whole body. From this point of view the relation of the human person to the world of men is one of dependence, which indicates his status as an individual within the species, and only able to achieve self-fulfilment within the whole body. Man, in fact, as an individual must fulfil himself only by becoming an integral part of a network of social interchanges: he cannot fulfil himself and yet live in isolation, because it is society which provides him with the conditions he needs in order to exist and develop. Fundamentally it is because it is incarnate and therefore subject to matter that the human person enters into this dependent relationship. Moreover, this dependence is not confined to the level of material needs that have to be satisfied, it exists also, and in a far deeper sense, at the level of the needs of the spirit. Man needs the help of other men to recognize himself as a person and to set all his powers in motion. In this connection we are thinking, it is true, of education, which is essentially an awakening of the personality. It is, for example, through education that the child gradually discovers his own existence and unique value within the family circle, and little by little he finds he is given responsibilities to discharge and these bring his freedom and generosity into play. But we are also thinking of love, which is the encounter and mutual recognition of two persons in which each freely offers himself to the other and reveals himself to himself by experiencing himself as the power to offer and therefore as a person. We might say that presence to oneself implies encounter with another.

It is true that, as universal in all human persons, human nature, since it embraces the particular individuals subject to it as members, passes beyond them. But the human person, being a spiritual reality, passes beyond and dominates human nature, and at this level, in its relation to the world of men, it is obviously a whole and a centre. Our analysis of the basic structure of the person made it clear that it is a totality, a universe in itself, in so far as it is a spiritual presence, possesses freedom, and is essentially related to God, of whom it is the indestructible likeness. It follows that the person in its essence can in no way be dependent on the species or on any society: it transcends and excels them, so that every society exists for the sake of, and in subordination to the person, which it can consider only as an end and never as a means, as a centre and not as a point on the circumference. One consequence becomes clear. It is that no human community can preserve its true character unless it respects what transcends it, that is that essential dignity of the human person which resides in its spirit, and spirit is indestructible and belongs to the realm of the absolute. There is evidently in human society an inherent state of tension. Of course, society should be naturally directed to the good of the human person, but it bears within it the seed of conflict owing to its tendency to regard the person only as a mere part, an objective element in the whole social body. By so doing society loses its own nature, since it loses and oppresses its centre, the person.

Another consequence follows. It is in a spiritual sense that the person is the centre of the whole, that is it rediscovers the whole in itself or, better, by its inward movement it lays hold of that principle of community which is based on the spiritual life whose nature it is to radiate and diffuse itself. The tendency of the person is to overflow by very reason of its perfections, and to communicate with others on the plane of knowledge and love. It is then that there is established between men that true communication which is communion, since it is established not through the body but through the spirit. The person is not only by nature the centre towards which everything converges, it is also the centre from which everything radiates. It is in this true communication between persons that humanity builds itself up and achieves fulfilment.

THE DEVELOPMENT OF THE PERSON

From its first appearance the human person is a unity but, as we have sufficiently stressed, it is rather an earnest of unity and a brittle one at that. Because of its incarnation it is always in danger of allowing itself to be submerged in the material world, and therefore has not only to defend itself against this snare but also to achieve the mastery of its spirit over matter. The human person has to build itself up, to give birth to itself in the forward movement of its being which it has received from God, and whose image it is. Herein lies the whole dignity of man and, at the same time, the source of the very great risks he undergoes. Thus we are able to understand that the "law" of the person consists in its spiritual and historical reality, in its being which is made for eternity but immersed in time.

Since we are dealing with a spiritual reality, we may begin by
seeing that the main lines of personal development seem to be
the following: (1) the *response* of the person to God who is closer
to him than he is to himself. The essential root of personality
must therefore be freedom. (2) An active welcome and an active
offering of self in which is expressed the "openness" of the
person based on its inwardness. It is through these characteristic acts of the spirit that the person's life and being are one
and the same thing. It is by responding, welcoming, offering
itself that the person truly becomes a person. It succeeds, that
is, in achieving true submission to God and the true mastery of
spirit over matter.

We shall therefore consider the development of the human
person as response, welcome and offering, in other words, in
those acts which can properly be carried out only by exercising
the virtues of freedom, knowledge and love which are proper
to the spirit.

THE PERSON IS RESPONSE, AND BECOMES
ITSELF BY RESPONDING

The inner nature of the person owes its form to the fact that
it is a being called by God to achieve, in the course of its life
history, that unification which is communion with the eternally
subsisting love of its creator. To this appeal, which comes forth
from God's Spirit, the person can respond only by an act of its
own spirit, which is freedom. Through this response man
becomes himself, and in the process he decides what direction
to give to his life and actions, he chooses to be what he is, a
person called to Love. We must therefore examine the nature
of this freedom which decides his destiny.

The idea of freedom at once implies absence of hindrance and
impediment: we speak of freedom to move about, freedom to
go where we like, freedom to trade, freedom to act. In the
absence of hindrance we are at the same time aware that a purpose is present, by which we mean that our will is directed

towards something we must do. This first approach should leave us with two aspects to be noted: absence of hindrance and presence of purpose which are moreover provided by our experience of the exercise of freedom, however elementary. This is enough for the moment to show us that freedom is first of all purpose capable of reaching its goal once any intervening obstacles have been removed. Since we are dealing with a characteristically mental activity, we must discover, beyond the many partial and changing purposes entertained by every human consciousness especially when a prey to distraction or diversion, some purpose expressive of the basic direction of our mind, a purpose of a spiritual kind transcending nature in its vital and instinctive aspects, a purpose underlying the dynamism of the will. If it is true that it is spiritual unity which constitutes personality and if it is also true that the human person is incomplete and unstable but yet moves towards its spiritual fulfilment, as we have already said, then we are now facing the deepest purpose of the human person, which is the achievement of the spiritual unity of its being. And if we remind ourselves that freedom is both the presence of purpose and the absence of hindrance, we may conclude that the essence of personal freedom is the power to fulfil oneself along the line of one's spiritual being, or the power, once the obstacles have been removed, to achieve the spiritual purpose which is the very form of our nature. In short, freedom is the "power to be".

This purpose or this "power to be" is inherent in us: we did not put it there ourselves. Freedom, indeed, presupposes human nature and consequently the purpose included in it. Because man has to become himself and, in a sense, to give birth to himself, he does not create himself. Self-creation is a contradiction in terms, since in order to create oneself one would have simultaneously to be and not to be: to be, in order to be able to act; not to be, in order to be able to enter into being. Moreover, when man exercises his freedom to become a particular person he gives effect to what he is but he does not create himself, since he is a human person from birth. In other words, to reverse the

Existentialist formula, existence does not precede essence[2]; man's "power to be" is a gift of God which he is powerless to change and from which he derives his fundamental meaning. It follows that freedom, which, as we have seen, is the power of self-fulfilment, can be accurately described as the acceptance of the invitation which constitutes its own inner nature and purpose: its task is to achieve and further the unfolding of this basic meaning, in other words to cooperate in God's plan for man.

Accordingly, when we say that freedom is the acceptance of the basic meaning of our spiritual nature, we understand it to be a choice. Man, in fact, although incapable of creating himself in the proper sense of the word, has this power of accepting or rejecting this basic meaning: it rests with him to decide for or against the essential purpose of his being, to determine his own destiny by refusing or by accepting what, in fact, he is. St Gregory of Nyssa says "our spiritual birth is the result of a free choice, and we are in some sort our own parents, making ourselves what we wish to be". This choice is possible and even necessary for the human person, for whom the capacity both of self-fulfilment and of choice is essential, with the result that his freedom may be accurately termed the power of choice placed at the service of the power of self-fulfilment.

The human person is choice because it is incomplete and for ever pursuing its goal in particular ends which fail to satisfy it. Human thought transcends human thoughts, the human will transcends human wishes. The human person cannot fail to be aware of the difference between what it is and what it becomes, between the ideal and the real. Hence it tends by its own

[2] Here we can do no more than refer to this principal theme of the Existentialist philosophy: existence precedes essence. By this is meant that man is not what he is obliged to be by the eternal and irrevocable fiat of an essence: he is what he has determined to be. Man, his destiny and the world are subject to the decision of the Ego. Sartre goes so far as to say that "Existentialism is a form of Humanism", and "Man is no more than his project, he exists only to the extent in which he realizes himself, he is no more than the totality of his acts, no more than the life he lives".

momentum to bridge this gap between its spiritual purpose
which is the basic drive towards its final goal, and its concrete
existence, between its desire to attain an absolute end and what
in fact it is able to achieve. The gap can only be bridged by an
act of choice, that is by freely making our own the basic
meaning of our existence.

From the psychological point of view it would seem that, for
the human person, the exercise of freedom is, as Sertillanges
expresses it, "a considered act of the will" and "a willed judgement". Prior to every form of act, man is a tendency, and since
he is a person this tendency is the primary will. Man wishes to
become himself, there is in him a will-to-be. What, we may ask,
is its objective? It is at this level that the deepest tendency of
personality is clarified by the intelligence, whose light must be
brought to bear before the voluntary act can be acceptable or
legitimate for the human person and thus transcend the order
of spontaneity and enter that of freedom. It is the intelligence
that supplies the will with a light and an object recognized as
perfect. The first stage in the advance towards freedom is the
judgement which refers particular ends to the ultimate end and
reveals the purpose of personality. The second stage is the
acceptance of this judgement by the will which assumes control
over it and implements it by bringing it to bear on the realm of
existence. This control of the judgement by the will is the fundamental basis of the free act. In the actual operation of this free
act three phases may therefore be distinguished. First there is
an original tendency consisting, in the case of a person, in a
will-to-be; secondly there is a process of reflection which pre-
pares the act and provides it with a rational foundation; and
finally there is a decision, that is, a choice. In other words, in
the free act intelligence and will are present as its constituents.
Hence we may say that freedom is the action of the spirit as a
whole and that it thus involves the whole person.

Human freedom is the freedom of a created being who is both
flesh and spirit. Two questions arise at this point. What is the
relation between created and divine freedom, and what are the

conditions under which man can live by his freedom, given the equivocal character of his being?

We have often to face this dilemma: if God exists, man cannot be free; if man is free, God cannot exist.[3] It is immediately obvious that the crux of this problem is to be found in the more or less implicit identification of God with man, and in the assertion that man's freedom, if it exists, must necessarily be absolute and self-engendered. This assertion of the absolute freedom of man is, as we have already emphasized, a contradiction when it is considered from the point of view of the basic purpose underlying the free act. It seems to us to rest essentially on a dubious notion of transcendence and of the relationships created beings have with it. If God can be conceived only by our immediately transferring to the realm of the absolute ideas that are valid in the world of contingency, thereby subjecting him to all the conditions of our human reality, it is certainly no longer easy to see what relations he can have with man other than that of master to slave, for both God and man would share the same nature, but the one would be infinite and the other necessarily finite: still more, if we take this situation to its extreme limit we finally recognize that God is both impossible and contradictory. But it is surely begging the question to assert, without further investigation, that God can only be conceived in terms of contingency, and to reject the experience which a man has in his relations with God on the grounds that it is unable to put us in touch with any genuinely existent reality. Here we can do no more than show not only that the relation between human and divine freedom is not contradictory, but that the latter creates the former. Indeed God, in creating all things, brings his action to bear on them in their capacity to exercise causality and in their active processes. It follows that he brings his action to bear on the act of human freedom, since this has its source in human existence of which

3 This dilemma is treated with great dialectical subtlety in the philosophy of Sartre, *L'Etre et le Néant* (English translation: *Being and Nothingness,* New York, Philosophical Library, 1953).

God is the cause. Nor can this freedom be exercised unless it is permeated by the divine causality that flows into it. Without this relationship it would not even exist, and far from destroying human freedom, it is its basis and gives it the power to become operative. It is at this point that we must gain an insight into the absolutely sovereign reality of God, who preserves all his creatures in the state in which he created them. Those are free whom he willed should be free, and those are bound by necessity whom he has willed should be so bound. God is the supreme reality in whom is no before or after, since he is his own eternal present. God strictly speaking does not foresee temporal events. Hence St Thomas says that for God there is nothing future, but he sees all things as he wills them (in particular the free decisions of the creature which as such are unforeseeable) at the very moment in which they take place either emerging spontaneously and freely or evolving according to predetermined necessity. There can therefore be no contradiction between Creative Freedom and created freedom, since they are not related as like to like but as creature to its transcendent creator.

Since man's freedom is the act of an incarnate spirit, it has to become itself and to fulfil itself, in other words to free itself, in order to render its action more intelligent and more flexible. Two conditions therefore—and we can only sketch their outline for the present—seem to us to be essential for the free act: the light of reason and mastery over oneself.

The free act, as we have said, is the act of the spirit as a whole performed jointly by the intelligence and the will, the former enlightening the latter as to its basic purpose and bringing projects face to face with motives. For this reason the first stage of an attempt at liberation strikes us as an attempt at clarity, all the more important in that the human person, because of its concrete situation, is always in danger of being inattentive and blind to the essential. The attempt at clarity is indeed ambivalent. It is an attempt to be present to oneself, and at the same time an attempt at concentration on what is fundamental for

the welfare of the person. The person becomes present to itself
to the degree in which it strives to elucidate itself, to understand
the deepest tendencies of its being, and to perceive itself as a
spiritual inwardness in such a way as to be able to master the
lowest as well as the highest of the motives which prompt it to
act, and to see reality not as it would like reality to be, but as it
is. As a result the person, being within itself, will be enabled to
pursue its quest for clarity by concentrating its attention on the
fundamental purpose of its being, to recognize the true nature
of that purpose, and to perceive finite goods through and with
reference to this purpose which constitutes the absolute in the
life of the person. It is by this means that the person gradually
weans itself from the seductions of finite ends and, by refusing
to succumb to them, avoids becoming fatally enslaved by them
and so destroying itself. Finally this effort to achieve clarity
should allow the person to solve the essential problem of its
existence: Why am I? For by being present to its inmost self the
person is enabled to know its centre of gravity, which consists
in free and loving response to God. Yet we know that this
response remains weak and insecure, like the person who makes
it, and is subjected to the tension between flesh and spirit. The
man who yields to instinctive impulse and the pressure of the
passions becomes a "carnal man", thereby losing his integrity
and his wholeness. As he is no longer one with himself because
of the loosening of the links between flesh and spirit, he can no
longer respond because he can no longer hear. His freedom,
yielding to the relative, is in some sort cut off from the source
which provided the impetus towards self-realization. Man
therefore is condemned to a long and painful struggle to
achieve the mastery of his spirit over his body, in other words,
that state of unity in which, when the life of the spirit rules and
assumes into itself the life of the flesh, man recognizes and loves
himself as a person.

THE PERSON FULFILS ITSELF BY ACCEPTANCE

The person, because it is spiritual inwardness, is a power of
acceptance, by which is meant not only the act of receiving but

the act of experiencing the presence of another person, of sharing his intimacy, of profiting from his abundance without depriving him of it, and of establishing an intellectual communion with him. Now it is precisely by the exercise of the intelligence that the human person can put into effect this faculty of acceptance, this capacity of becoming all things and thereby becoming more itself. For the person, acceptance is one of the principal means of existing and consequently of becoming itself, since the act of acceptance is a spiritual act, an act of spiritual presence.

We are here concerned not with a psychological description of the acts of cognition but merely with an indication of the spiritual value of the act of intelligence as the fulfilment of the person in his faculty of acceptance based on his inwardness. We shall show knowledge as "openness", as presence and as existence, and consequently as a guarantee of the progress of the person in its spiritual life.

The primary characteristic of the intellect is that it is "open". It addresses itself always to the whole of reality, by which is meant the totality of being, which it seeks to appropriate. Prior to all act, the intellect is inwardly an inclination or opening out towards that which is. This acceptance is, from its very principle, universal, since everything that exists is true, in the exact sense that all created things are the thought of God informing existence, and that consequently everything that is is intelligible because it was created by God. The universality of this principle of acceptance is a necessary consequence of that inwardness or non-material nature of the spirit which constitutes the core of personality. A person is the more "open" the less it is immersed in matter which is the principle of individuation. Hence the thought-provoking expression of St Thomas: "Now the power of God in knowing is as great as his actuality in existing"; that is as great as his absolute immateriality.

This universal acceptance or "openness" to the totality of being which characterizes the primary urge of the intelligence has for its object the inclusion of the known in the knower. This inclusion is to be understood in the most active and spiritual sense. For an object to be known, it is not enough that it is present to my consciousness, it must be in it, becoming in a way myself: in Bergson's words, "we know and understand only what we can somehow reinvent". The intellect, in fact, admits the object to the closest intimacy, achieving the highest degree of unity of two in one, since by knowledge the intellect, precisely owing to its immateriality and spirituality, has the power of becoming the object without either intellect or object suffering any change. In the act of knowing, both object and subject remain unchanged in the existence that is theirs by nature, while at the same time they become one. It is this process that constitutes genuine communication, which consists not in confusion but in inward union, whereby the person while universalizing himself achieves a greater degree of inwardness to himself by enlarging his spiritual existence. Knowledge must be considered in terms of existence, since it is concerned with what is the most existent, because the most spiritual, reality. And this leads to another profound truth.

When it is achieved, knowledge is no mere appearance but a means of enriching and perfecting the knowing subject, of realizing the highest potentialities of the person. This is strictly true of consciousness. It is indisputable that knowledge awakens us to consciousness of self, and that this union of subject and object always involves a clearer apprehension of the self. Thus sleep cuts us off from what is not ourselves, and consequently in a sense from ourselves: we should, in fact, be entirely cut off from ourselves did we not carry over into our sleeping state some element of other things. But we must go further if we are to show that the person is fulfilled by intellectual acceptance. To know is to exist, not with the limited existence appropriate to a material being, but with the unlimited existence appropriate to the spirit, in which the subject by "becoming" others enhances its own identity. It follows that knowledge is the surest means not only of knowing ourselves as existing but also of existing at the highest possible level. We

expand our personality to its true dimensions by maintaining
ourselves at the deepest level of existence, which may be defined
as inwardness, and by insisting on communication through
knowledge, which implies keeping our personalities "open".
Hence St Thomas, following Aristotle, says that the act of
knowing is a life, and is all that is most perfect in life.

Again, it is knowledge that reveals in its own order the
relation between the person and God. On the one hand that
"incarnate idea" which a thing is derives its reality solely from
the Thought underlying it;[4] on the other hand the pursuit of
the truth, which is the intellect's primary urge, is a proof of its
innate attachment to infinite Being and sovereign Truth. Therefore contemplation is rightly esteemed as the highest form of
the life of the mind, and as the activity most characteristic of
the person. Here we are concerned with the dignity of the mind,
which not only is a perfection analogically similar to an attribute of deity, but is also capable of knowing God and of being
thereby united to him in the deepest intimacy. Genuine "deiform" contemplation is undoubtedly that inspired by the love
of God displayed by the saints, for it is not the rational faculty
that makes a spiritual contemplative but the purity of charity.
Nevertheless, just as in the natural order contemplation is the
crown of life, so in the supernatural order the clearest proof
of love is the contemplation of God, which renders action
consistent and fruitful.

Acceptance, the fine flower of the understanding, is the true
fulfilment of the person, because it consists in "openness",
presence and existence. Nevertheless it is subject to the necessary limitations of the human person in his act of intelligence.
Thus the understanding is controlled by the structure of human
personality. It is sufficiently disengaged from matter to be able
to know, but in the act of knowing it remains partly dependent
on matter, a circumstance which explains its slow advance

---

[4] "The knower knows God implicitly in the knowledge of the object,
since nothing is knowable except by similarity to the First Truth" (St
Thomas, *De Veritate*, Qu. 22, art. 2, ad 1).

towards knowledge, and the dissociation of object and subject which characterizes it from the outset. The understanding, because it is a faculty of a being who is both flesh and spirit, is influenced by the fleshly element present in all human beings. It is affected, for example, by the state of our bodies and our vital instincts. By the very fact of this situation the human understanding, in order to safeguard the acceptance and presence which characterize it, has to set in operation a deep-seated form of attention-consciousness, and a profound honesty-sincerity. The burden of his material individuality draws man towards an attitude of inattention and distraction in the etymological sense of the word (*distrahere*): that is, he is separated from himself and is consequently less receptive and "open". This absence from oneself shows itself in a twilight state which finally culminates in a loss of contact with reality. It is not that reality grows more opaque, but that the human mind through lack of attention loses flexibility and insight: failure to attend leads to an imperfect perception of reality. On the other hand if, by a process of adjustment appropriate to the human personality, we make ourselves present to ourselves, we shall find ourselves in a state of receptivity that will admit us to the heart of reality. Pascal said that an increase in intelligence brings with it a greater awareness of uniqueness. A man who is present to himself, who actualizes his spiritual inwardness, will not stop short at mere appearances but will be able to penetrate the depths of reality, since "all things conceal a certain mystery, all things are veils concealing God" (Pascal, *4th Letter to Mlle de Roannez*).

Finally, receptivity requires an effort at sincerity, which in this context means intellectual sincerity. The fact is that in the human act of knowing, subject and object never completely interpenetrate; and this incomplete union is a sign of the mind's search for the truth: a truth which we apprehend is always a challenge to further inquiry. Experience teaches us that the human mind is prone to be content with partial truths which it complacently accepts as absolute. This error not only

debases the partial truths by dissociating them from the absolute Truth, but destroys the receptivity of the mind, since the
imposition of conditions and consequently of limitations on the
mind's receptivity necessarily is in fact to deprive it of every
spiritual characteristic.

This twofold effort imposed by its concrete situation will
then enable the mind to become the instrument of the human
person's fulfilment, the instrument, that is, both of the most
universal receptivity possible and of the most intimate presence.

THE PERSON REALIZES ITSELF BY SELF-SACRIFICE

Whereas knowledge comes about when the known is within
the knower, and is therefore essentially an act of welcome, the
exercise of the will is the result of the attraction of the beloved
for the lover, and this attraction culminates in an outward
movement from the self. In this situation we no longer speak of
the object being present in its intelligibility to the subject, but of
an inclination or movement which is properly described as an
offering. This impulse, in fact, is not instinctual, it is that of a
spirit freely giving itself to someone other than itself whose
inherent value it recognizes and to which it offers itself un-
reservedly. Love is precisely this offering of ourselves which
moves us towards others. It is, as St Augustine called it, our
weight, which conveys us wherever we go. The will, which is
love in action, is consequently both the attraction of being in
so far as it has a certain degree of perfection, and the generous
response to that attraction. From this circumstance there
follow two illuminating consequences. The first concerns the
ultimate orientation of the will, and here we return to the profound meaning of the vocation of man as "the image of God".
Since the object of the will is being in so far as it is complete, it
follows that the will is drawn primarily towards the perfection
not of that existence which is limited but of Existence itself in
its supreme actuality. In the second place it follows that the
will does not create the perfection which attracts it, but in the

light of intelligence responds to that good which is ever present to it and is the true reflection of absolute Goodness.

Even a limited experience reveals that this outward movement of the will towards the object, in which the act of love consists, can take two directions, one of which demonstrates the genuineness of our offering and guarantees the fulfilment of our personality. Either the lover loves the beloved for the sake of and as the beloved, and this is the love of friendship which wishes the friend to have life and every other good thing, or else the lover loves the beloved for the lover's or for some other good, in which case love becomes covetousness or possession. This classic distinction at once reveals the two kinds of relationship between lover and beloved. Desire or covetousness aims at supplying a need: the love of friendship, on the other hand, contains the necessary relationship between two persons. In other words, and this is the essential point, when we use the terms "love of friendship" and "love of desire", we only do so with reference to being which attracts us. It follows that the love of desire can be directed only to a being which is *in* itself but lacks spiritual inwardness, whereas the love of friendship can be directed only to a being which is *for* itself, since it is loved for itself and appreciated as an ultimate goal of love. To be aware of this relation of love to being is to make certain of the reality of the object towards which we are impelled. We know, of course, that it is always possible to love someone in order to make use of him, but this results in the loss of his dignity and personal value, we love him merely as an object (*en soi*) and not as a subject in his own right (*pour soi*). The love of friendship brings out the characteristics of personality, since it proceeds from one person to another. It is the expression of the "open" nature of the spirit.

The goal at which love aims is a superior mode of existence, since the lover strives for the closest possible union with the beloved. In the love of desire, as contrasted with the spiritual depths of the love of friendship, affection takes the shape of the object loved in order to grasp and possess it, whereas in the love of friendship there is a living union in which—and this is love's supreme act—the will of the lover adapts itself to that of the beloved: the lover, so to speak, lives by the will of the beloved and loves him as if he were himself. This is expressed in St Augustine's grief at the death of his friend: "Yes, I felt that his soul and mine were but one soul in two bodies. Wherefore I loathed life, and wished to live no more, for I had lost one half of myself" (*Confessions*, Book 4, vi, II).

In order to express the strength of this union we may borrow the extremely concrete word *convivium* used by St Thomas to refer to love as a life shared, a life of union. In modern usage this word has the meaning of a "common meal" which is the type and symbol of all forms of communal life. The union demanded by love is a life lived together, a true union since love aims at presence. In the love of friendship the lover and the beloved desire to be no longer two but one, to achieve the closest possible intimacy of existence; the goal of love is the communion in being of two existences, a communion in which "I" and "he" are replaced by "I" and "you". It is therefore that close community of "you" and "me" in "us" which may be called the colloquy of two persons offering themselves to each other. G. Marcel says, "I say 'you' only to a person who can answer; nor does it matter what the answer is, even if it is nothing but a silence full of understanding. Where no answer is possible, there is room for the 'he'." In this "we", each party finds himself by giving himself, for the union of love is neither a confusion of substances nor an actual identification of wills, which would result in the destruction rather than the fulfil-ment of the lover and the beloved. Really to love someone is to fulfil his personality: in love the person finds itself again. At this level we must point out that we meet once more the characteristic mark of the person, who by universalizing him-self goes still further into himself. And we meet once more the law of genuine communication, since every lover finds himself again in those to whom he gives and for whom he offers him-self.

But we must go further than this, for though the love of friendship goes out towards persons it can go inward to myself as a person; and love for another then becomes love of oneself. This seeming paradox is not a glorification of egoism, but is the very basis of all genuine love of others. Love of oneself is contained in love of others, which in short it guarantees, and this means that it is fundamentally rooted in what we have called the personality, which we described in the formula: the more interior the person becomes, the more "open" it is. In fact, to love oneself is to love one's being in all its dimensions, its vocation, its likeness to God and in its true nature as a being called by God. To love oneself is to be fully inward to oneself, to desire to penetrate one's own depths, whose centre of gravity is God, and consequently to share in God's all-embracing love. Furthermore, by loving that which makes me what I am I shall thereby be enabled to understand the importance of that other person who confronts and calls me. I shall understand that he is like me and shares the same mysterious reality. I shall be certain of following my own impulse which is in direct relation with my own inwardness. The deeper that inwardness becomes the more "open" shall I be. The more my love projects me outside myself, the more will my inwardness increase: this is the dialectic of love, whose progress it guarantees. The familiar injunction to love one's neighbour as oneself thus acquires a deeper significance. It means that just as we love ourselves as persons, so ought we to love others as persons, to respect their value, their freedom and inner being. Moreover, the less we esteem ourselves the more we lose sight both of ourselves and of the meaning of others, whom we are tempted to treat as objects or means, an error which amounts to a form of sin. Consequently no man can achieve the union of love unless he accepts and loves himself as a person.

This existential unity brought about by love reaches its greatest height and perfection in the love of God, which is at the same time the principle and the goal of the will's impulse towards being, since it is from God that all things proceed and towards God that all things gravitate. This union, says St Thomas, this fellowship and familiar converse of man with God, is that supreme perfection of love to which man aspires according to his condition and to the best of his ability. This union, however—and for the moment we can only draw attention to it in passing—can be accomplished only in the supernatural order, that is by the free gift of God's grace which extends and develops the primordial movement of our being. This was the call addressed to our first parents. It is the very basis of the vocation which constitutes the human person, the grace which succeeds in bridging the gap between the nature of the creator and that of his creation. Thanks to it, even on earth man lives his life with God, and can actually, though dimly, experience the presence of God, whom he can contemplate as the source of Charity.

As this offering, which love is, is rooted in the person of which it is the expression, it is necessarily bound by its condition and follows the same slow path towards personalization. This impulse of our being has the same characteristics as our person, and in it the same faults are recognizable. Our love, springing as it does from an incarnate person, can never be an entirely forward movement, a complete fusion of two spirits. It is true that love proceeds from spirit to spirit, but in the process it has to pass through a body which is a barrier and an obstacle. Our love is mediated by signs, which, however much we may invest them with the presence of the spirit, necessarily remain ambiguous, since, being both material and spiritual, their meaning may be distorted. We are dealing with the impulse of a being who is both body and spirit. Consequently we are aware of the risk, in this as in other respects, of polarizing our offering on the material aspect. It is always in man's power to destroy love, thereby denying himself by enclosing himself in an egocentric love.

By response, acceptance and sacrifice the person, bringing into play the highest spiritual forces of freedom, understanding and will, advances in line with his own inwardness towards self-fulfilment. This advance, however, is that of an incarnate person who is both body and mind, in time and eternity. It is at the point where this incarnation and this spiritual progress meet that the person becomes part of history and lives the story of his own life. And so we reach the synthesis and conclusion of our investigations into the essential structure of man. We conclude that man, as an ontologically realized unity of body and mind, is because of this structure an evolving, and therefore a historical unity. History for a person is simply the progress of which it is the author, and which consists in the advent of the spirit: it is the process by which the person becomes itself. Yet since human personality acquires no fullness, and does not even exist except in its relation to God, we begin to see that its history, or its spiritual development, will assume its full significance in the response made to the absolute, a response which may take the form of choice or refusal. At this point begins the drama of man's total destiny.

PART II

MAN FALLEN AND REDEEMED

So far we have attempted to explain the mystery of man in his essential structure, in his spiritual dimensions as a being created in the image and likeness of God. But this optimistic vision is sadly contradicted by the facts of everyday life. In actual fact man is a frail creature, threatened from every quarter. He finds himself conditioned by the conflict between flesh and spirit, by the struggle against all that attacks his mastery over himself. We may say with Pascal: "When I consider the blindness and misery of man, when I contemplate the dumb universe and man, bereft of light, left to his own resources and, as it were, lost in this corner of the universe, ignorant of who put him there, of what is his allotted task and what will become of him when he comes to die, and incapable of any knowledge, I feel the same terror as a man transported in his sleep to a terrifying desert island, and waking without knowing where he is and with no way of escape."

It is now our task to follow this painful path of human history in order to discover whether human existence has any meaning, or whether it ends inevitably in ultimate absurdity. We have to consider whether the question of man's nature permits of any answer other than a scepticism that breeds death.

CHAPTER IV

LOST UNITY:
FROM ANGUISH TO PEACE

We have seen that in the beginning the goodness of God called to the intimacy of his love a privileged creature endowed by divine grace with complete unity. But what has become of this image of God? Everywhere we see raised against it a kind of challenge, consisting in the rejection of the eternal. Contemporary art, which is no mere make-believe but the expression of a world in torment, seems in certain of its manifestations to launch a fierce attack against the face of man. The theatre, the novel, painting and sculpture seem more often than not to portray the confusion of a mankind bereft of all inwardness. And worse still, the technical revolution and every example of scientific advance seem to bring in their train like a satellite the depersonalization of man and his reduction to an instrument or tool. Thus it is possible for Albert Camus to point out that "the seventeenth century was the century of mathematics, the eighteenth that of physics, and the nineteenth that of biology. Our own twentieth century is the century of fear." The question arises in the minds of all of us: in a world where the spirit of man asserts itself daily by some new discovery, whence comes this agonizing terror, this anguish which chokes the natural spring of human life? We suffer within the inmost recesses of our whole being, from our awareness of our condition and situation in the world, "the natural misfortune of our fragile and mortal state, which is so wretched that nothing can console us when we allow our minds to dwell on it." Although man is a unity, since he was created in the image of God, his unity appears to be so disrupted that it is no longer possible to recognize in it the stamp of his creator.

ONE OR MANY?

"What a monster is man . . . the repository of truth, a sink of doubt and error, the glory and scum of the universe" (Pascal, *Pensées*, No. 434). Human nature is at bottom a tangle of contradictions. No sooner does man acquire self-consciousness and at least partial responsibility for his own existence, than he seems to be subjected to a double movement which makes him in some sort aware of the ambiguity of his being, and brings home to him the paradox of his complex situation resulting from his partly bodily, partly spiritual condition. We have already remarked that human nature, which is a unity involving tension and strife, contains the seeds of conflict and dissolution which may result in genuine wounds. Because of his complex condition, man runs the risk of giving preference to the carnal and temporal aspect of his being, without for all that succeeding in suppressing its spiritual aspect: as one of Dostoevsky's heroes says: "The fact is there are two people within me, and this terrifies me. It is as though one's double were at one's side." These dangers are rooted in our nature which is flesh and spirit, in our vocation which operates in freedom, and in our basic limitation as created beings. They are dangers which really confront each one of us every day.

One fact is immediately obvious: we find ourselves in a given situation; we are a nexus of relations both in the universe and in human society.

We are aware of ourselves as situated within this universe which surrounds and includes us. It is true that no sooner are we awakened to existence by the impact of the world upon us, than we become aware that we are distinct from this world yet at the same time identical with it, since we share with it the same mysterious fact of existence. We are on friendly terms with the universe in which we are set to work not only to draw out of it our means of subsistence but also to change, humanize and spiritualize it. Nevertheless the ambivalence of our relation to the world becomes immediately apparent.

When our consciousness awakens in the universe, certain strange limitations force themselves on our attention, and we soon become aware of an element of weakness and frailty which we cannot avoid by any kind of escape mechanism. We know that we risk allowing ourselves to be mastered by the very forces which we imagined were under our control, and today this risk seems to be becoming a painful reality under the pressure of a science and a technology apparently divorced from all that is deepest in human nature. It may well be that the "cosmic suicide" foretold by the German philosopher Nikolaus Hartmann will actually come to pass, since scientific power by itself is powerless to avert it. F. Mounier has suggested that one day man's denial of man may end in the insanity of man's destruction by man. "Contemporary man thinks himself absurd, whereas he is perhaps merely insane. I am terrified of the madman who, confronted by two buttons one of which will bring universal prosperity while the other will produce the final atomic explosion, imagines that the scientist or his agent will be guided by the pure light of science to press the button of salvation rather than the button of death." It is a striking paradox, revealing the profound lack of harmony between man and the universe. The greater man's mastery of nature, the greater seems his fear of her. His relation to the universe has become centred on struggle: he is the master, but is in danger of becoming a slave. He stands above the visible world as a worker of wonders and its master and lord, he bends its secret forces to his own use, but such is his subjection that he finally surrenders to the combined forces of matter and is incapable of perceiving any possibility of certain or even possible revenge. What was originally a fraternal harmony seems to have become a deep-seated dissension.

Social life exhibits the same paradox. It is undeniable that man cannot attain his full stature in solitude: "No man is an island." Our very being impels us towards union and communion with our fellow men. We depend upon each other not only in the struggle for material existence but more genuinely on the spiritual plane, in the interchange of knowledge and love. Thus we know that our true and personal existence is based on our relations with our fellow men. But we soon find that there is a reverse side to the medal. Although we are capable of the noblest feelings and the most fruitful sacrifices in the interests of what is good and for the sake of love, we are equally prone to spitefulness and selfishness which are the ruin of all love. Moreover it can happen that our love of mankind is not returned but betrayed, and that our deepest feelings are misrepresented. "It is through Beelzebub, the prince of the devils, that he casts the devils out" (Luke 11. 15). Men ought to aim to become a community of brothers sharing the same life and ideals, but in politics and economics the class war is an undeniable fact, war between nations has become endemic, and everywhere man is often the prey of man. In fact, the history of human relationships seems to be no more than the history of human conflict. Social life, under the impulse of ideology, is no longer a society of men but a means of reducing men to the status of tools who are free only to belong to the movement that enslaves them. Sartre was right in saying that "the essence of the relations between conscious beings is not *mitsein* but conflict", or in the famous last words of *Huis Clos*, "Hell is other people".

We experience the same feeling when we turn from the most visible sphere of our existence, that of human relations, to the dynamic reality of our inner existence. Moreover, the sense of conflict which man experiences in his relation to the world and to his fellow men springs from the conflict within himself. In all our actions we are conscious of a strange inadequacy deriving from a feeling of impotence combined with a genuine but never fulfilled aspiration. It is undeniable that our ideals are never realized, and that our will encounters insuperable obstacles and is impaired by incurable weaknesses. In all his actions man may seem to aim at the infinite: in the words of Fichte, "we can love nothing unless we regard it as eternal". Nevertheless he often rests content with the finite: in his pursuit of the infinite he is like a child vainly chasing his shadow. Our sympathies are weak, our desires fickle. We greedily seek to possess people and things, but when our hopes are realized we often remain hungry and unsatisfied. Our nostalgia for the eternal is accompanied by inconstancy and a great capacity of forgetfulness, so that we may say with St Paul, "it is not the good my will prefers, but the evil my will disapproves, that I find myself doing" (Rom. 7. 19).

An inexplicable and incurable breach appears to break human nature in two at its very core. At death a human being becomes "defunct", that is he no longer has any part to play in human affairs. Hence the bitter words of Achilles. "Speak not to me of death. I had rather be a farm-labourer and toil for a wage, or a poor man who has hardly enough to eat, than to be captain of the army of the dead who are no more." As we grow old we realize that we are creatures born to die, and from our failures, partings and our own increasing years the thought is borne in upon us that life may be after all no more than waiting for death. Nevertheless this very experience derives its stability from the birth of a profound desire to transcend the bounds of space and time and to aim at a superior state of being, in other words, a desire not to die. At this point we are thrown back on the mystery of human existence, and are driven to ask the fundamental question whether life is worth living or not.

Conflict and suffering in man are caused by the inner contradiction involved in this dialectic of subjection and transcendence, weakness and strength, denial and affirmation. This conflict seems to be rooted in the limited nature of our being, in its contingency, in the fact that we bear in us the mark of our original "nothingness" and possess no kind of necessary being. Yet this does not take us to the heart of the problem. The conflict is not merely between men confronting one another and conscious of their disparity and divided selves: it is surely the confrontation of man with God. The realization of our ambiguous situation must therefore lead to a closer examination of the drama of existence in the concrete.

ANGUISH AND ANXIETY

We feel ourselves to be vulnerable with respect to our existence and our value as individuals. The consciousness of our contingence produces a profound disturbance within us. For contingence is not something external; it is at the heart of our existence, since it defines its very character. Furthermore, we realize that it is not a part of human existence that is threatened, but existence itself that is challenged. In fact, the consciousness of our ambiguity brings home to us the possibility that our being may disintegrate and vanish in the universe and in the world of men.

From the realization of this possibility there springs the emotion known as anguish. Here we approach one of the main themes of contemporary philosophy as it confronts the human tragedy. It is the central theme of Existentialism, which regards anguish as the fundamental experience of contingent existence and as the hall-mark of authentic existence. This experience is exceptional only because men take refuge from it in distractions which mask reality.

The victim of anguish is acutely aware both of the conflict in which his existence is at stake, and of the possibility of his downfall. Hence it has been justly observed that the closest parallel to anguish is the sense of dizziness. A man attacked by dizziness seems rigid with fear, torn between the reality of fear and the desire to overcome it. The question arises whether man, conscious of his unstable and threatened existence in the world, is condemned beyond hope of reprieve to be the prey of this dizziness and anguish. Can it be that man is essentially "a despairing consciousness", and that anguish is the sole and basic experience of his contingent existence? In other words, is man driven to assert the absurdity and radical nonsense of his existence, since this anguish he experiences imprisons him in his state of despair and disintegration? Is human existence doomed to defeat?

These questions are answered in the affirmative by Heidegger and Sartre, the two leading exponents of modern Existentialism. Without going into detail we may observe that each of them, though from different points of view, singles out anguish as the absolute criterion of "authentic existence", and so are led to reject any belief in a genuinely transcendent being, and to assert the radical absurdity of existence. For Heidegger it seems that the dominating factor is the idea of the abandonment or forsakenness to which we are condemned in a world where we seem to have been literally thrown with no choice in the matter, with the result that we are always conscious of our isolation. We are strangers in the world. "We feel ourselves floating in the void, sinking in the midst of chaos." In other words our presence in the world is inexplicable and absurd, and the consciousness of our situation begets in us the anguish and fear which are the very essence of all that genuinely exists.

In his novel *Nausea* Sartre gives the following description of the experience of existing. "Existence is not something which can be thought of at a distance. It must assault us, fasten on us, crush our hearts like some foul monster." "To exist is simply to be there ... contingency is not a pretence, a mere outward appearance which we can dispel, it is the absolute, and therefore perfectly gratuitous ... not one of us has the least reason for being there, every confused and vaguely uneasy creature that exists feels itself unwanted by its fellows ... every existing creature is born without reason, continues to exist out of sheer weakness, and dies by chance." Therefore existence disgusts and nauseates us simply by showing us what it is, irrational and meaningless. It is at this point that man falls headlong into anguish, which is that state in which we discover the facts of authentic existence. It is true that Heidegger and Sartre concede that the feeling of anguish is exceptional, but all the same it constitutes the only true texture of life. Their analysis of existence as embedded in this experience of anguish leads them to reject more or less explicitly any transcendent being and to assert a radical absurdity. Man is in every respect alone, a prey to the anguish caused by the total contingency of his existence, deprived of any consolation other than his own lucidity. He yearns for what is impossible and contradictory, he longs to be one with himself but never succeeds. Sartre goes so far as to say that "humanity is condemned to suffer by its very being, since it comes into being for ever haunted by a totality which it is and yet cannot be, since it cannot become 'In-itself' (a subject) without destroying itself as the 'For-itself' (an object). It is therefore by nature a despairing consciousness unable to pass beyond its state of misery."

We have given this rapid summary of existentialist philo-sophy so that we can now ask the question whether the ambiguity and fragmentation inherent in human existence must inevitably result in an anguish and absurdity enclosing mankind within itself in an existence without hope. In our opinion the answer is no. There seems no reason to assign a special status to the rarely experienced emotion of anguish and to assert that it alone is authentic, unless it has already been decided that the only way men can avoid a commonplace exist-ence is by being unhappy. But this is to beg the question. As a matter of fact the experience of anguish is from the outset implicit in Existentialism as a solution of the problem of the meaning of existence, a solution, that is, which postulates the radical contingency and total absurdity of existence. But this is an *a priori* solution and so purely gratuitous. After all, to exalt anguish is expressly to dismiss all other forms of experience, and to dismiss them without inspection as unauthentic. Thus it is characteristic of Sartre to say, in *Nausea*: " 'A meaning of sorts': the word set my nerves on edge. I could never under-stand it even if I stayed leaning on the railings for a hundred and seven years. I had learned all I could ever know about existence."

Our account of the sense of the ambiguity of existence shows that man is subject to two conflicting experiences. On the one hand is the uneasiness inseparable from the realization of his status and situation in the universe and in human society, on the other is the impulse to transcend if possible his limitations, the desire to make contact with the eternal on which he can found his hopes. It follows that the emotion most closely resembling this experience is anxiety, which is the convergence, in a single consciousness, of suffering, which is fear, and hope, which is joy. We suffer because of our limitations and our knowledge that everything is transitory and must have an end. We hope because hope is an impulse rooted in our nature urging us towards that which can give us self-fulfilment, supreme happiness and the realization of our aspirations. This indissoluble union of suffering and hope expresses itself in that dissatisfaction with ourselves which may become the active principle of a dynamic force impelling the soul to seek transcendence. We may therefore accept Gabriel Marcel's definition of anxiety as "the movement whereby the human soul renouncing all self-complacency and also all attachment to material things, frees itself from self and, in a sense, goes forward to meet grace". It follows that the recognition of our divided nature ceases to be a stumbling-block or a collapse into absurdity, and becomes a means whereby man is, as it were, lifted above his fears and can move towards him who is able to grant him peace, for he is Love. In short, anxiety is the operation of grace in the souls of God's creatures.

Viewed in these terms, anxiety may be described as the readiness to accept the light and shade inseparable from the ambiguity of human nature, and to enter on this path that opens on to the eternal: in other words, man must accept the mysterious conditions of his existence. Whereas anguish is egocentric, genuine anxiety is a way out, a call, it is a desire for a higher form of being for it sees that our agony and suffering have a meaning. It is, as it were, the inner spring of our progress and transcendence. In this connection we may cite the anxiety of the saints which is the "peace" of the Gospel, because it is both a humble acknowledgment of weakness and an ineradicable conviction of the power and the goodness of God. Anxiety becomes a living force only when rooted in the absolute value of the love of God.

Anxiety also shows that, in the complications and uncertainties of our life, we long, however obscurely, for unity. It is the impulse to harmonize our lives, to assume our contradictory experiences into a unification and simplification of the heart. It is a sign of man's search for unity. Many writers, from Rilke to Saint-Exupéry, have equated this quest with the nostalgia for childhood. Man, in his anxiety, seems to be seeking the marvellous simplicity of the age of innocence, the purity which has been lost amid the storms of life. But this nostalgia for childhood is often no more than a poetic and sterile regret. Indeed, on the one hand this childhood purity is often merely the natural innocence of a creature hitherto shielded from the world. On the other hand to hanker for a past however pure is to choke the springs of the life of the spirit and to turn it in on itself. Accordingly anxiety is concerned not with a regressive unity, but with a unity open to the world and capable of development, a unity which resists every centrifugal tendency, and a consecration of the spirit in its relation to the absolute, which is its source and its goal.

Consequently, we reach the conclusion that this quest for unity, which is the foundation of anxiety, consists in choice, choice not of the centrifugal which keeps our life at surface level, but of God who, because he is Love, can alone make us one, and whose life in us can guarantee our invulnerability throughout the distracting vicissitudes of life and the wounds of existence, and so give us grounds for hope. It should be noted that this choice, which is inspired from within by a free acceptance of the fact of our contingency, consists in handing back our freedom to him who gave it us, not as we return a material object, but by an act of liberty freely present in the gift of ourselves. It is by this act that man achieves the unity which is peace; for, in the words of Dante, "in his will is our peace".

We are now in a position to see that the antithesis of this choice is disobedience to God's will, that is sin; and this consideration leads us to the heart of our problem, to the source of our contradictions and distractions, and to the mysterious origin of our struggles and suffering. Psychology and psychoanalysis are justified in looking for the centre of our complexes in the unconscious and the subconscious, but the truths of religion go deeper still. Religion teaches us that the real struggle is waged between the flesh and the spirit, and that, in Dostoevsky's words, "it is the devil who wrestles with God, and the field of battle is the human heart".

"YOU YOURSELVES WILL BE LIKE GODS"

Man's first choice was his first defeat, and "it was through one man that guilt came into the world; and, since death came owing to guilt, death was handed on to all mankind by one man" (Rom. 5. 12).

Revelation leads us to the inmost cause of all our contradictions and sufferings, and gives rise to our anguish or anxiety. Called as he was to share the life of his creator, the first man should have responded freely to God's free invitation. His loving intercourse with God could only have been the free union of his will with the uncreated will.

> When men first came to be, it was God made them, and, making them, left them to the arbitrament of their own wills; yet giving them commandments to be their rule. Those commandments if thou wilt observe, they in their turn shall preserve thee, and give thee warrant of his favour. It is as though he offered thee fire and water, bidding thee take which thou wouldst; life and death, blessing and curse, man finds set before him, and the gift given thee shall be the choice thou makest (Ecclus 15. 14–18).

But the choice made by the first man, which involved all his descendants, was to reject the absolute of love; so true is it that he can make his fundamental choice only by confronting the absolute. The bare statement "you yourselves will be like gods"

(Gen. 3. 5) carries us to the origin of the tragedy of mankind, to the heart of all the refusals which recur throughout human history, and to the heart of all the atheisms for which the death of God only means that man can live.

The story of Genesis is a striking demonstration of the depth and extent of sin. For the fact is that this rejection of God shatters the unity of man and his fraternal relations with the universe because it strikes at the point of intersection in his being created in God's own image and likeness. Sin not only contaminates but wounds existence, because it has no existence other than that given it by a spirit: hence sin is made powerful enough to undo and, as it were, to mutilate the very work of God.

We are now in a position to understand the vast repercussions of the sin of the first man. On the one hand, he was granted a privileged status as a creature raised by grace to fellowship with God; on the other hand he was the origin of the entire human race of which he was to be the progenitor. Therefore, since sin has no existence other than that given it by a spirit, it is clear that its effects are commensurate with the dignity of this spirit; sin is more active and powerful in proportion to the higher degree in the order of the spirit of him who commits it. Furthermore, since trust in God involves the surrender of the whole personality to God's own personal witness, it would seem to follow that the disobedience of Adam amounted to a real act of infidelity committed through lack of trust in God's word. It would then be the sin which destroys the supernatural order at the deepest level and the first of those denials to which the devil always tempts the most powerful human minds in their abandonment to pride. By this denial nature expressed a preference and chose its own limits. Although created only to receive all that God has prepared for her, she cut across that purpose through a self-sufficiency rooted in pride. Thus from the beginnings of human history we are faced with the religious mystery of the harmony between nature and grace, and of the necessity of accepting what God offers us. This is a perennial problem confronting human pride, which seeks to lay down its own standards of wisdom and virtue, and thinks itself capable of attaining supreme happiness by the assertion of its autonomy and through the exercise of its own powers. Throughout the centuries, in varying tones, the cry of revolt is heard: "Man's God is Man!"

The first man (and with him all his descendants) fell back upon himself, was satisfied to be self-contained, and, by refusing to admit his status of creature, turned the forward impulse of his whole being inwards. Henceforward he is "out of centre" and blind to his true centre of gravity, the source of his unity freely bestowed on him by the goodness of God. The tragic consequence of sin is that, through his projection of a reflection of the light that deifies on to what is finite and his hazarding all on the self-sufficiency of the creature, the person loses himself in his attempt to find himself apart from his relation to the absolute. As soon as man turns his back on God, whose creation and image he is, he risks losing himself in the loss of the principle of his unity.

Sin inflicted a deep wound on the human person. In the words of J. Mouroux: "The sin of Adam involved the human race in a cleavage between creation and adoption: God continues to give life, but no longer his life. Every man born into the world is no longer all that God wishes him to be. . . . Though man's essence remains intact, henceforward his nature is wounded. He has no longer the power to move towards his predestined goal, he is too weak and blind to endure the divine presence which is henceforward his nourishment and true delight. He is incapable of that act of union with God which would restore him to life, he can only fall back upon himself, powerless and imprisoned within himself, shut off from his fellows and from God." Sin denotes a triple breach in the threefold relations which constitute the human person—his relation to God, to men and to the universe. This fact gives us an insight into the ambiguity of our condition and our situation.

When man rejects God's will he rejects God. He also rejects

his love, since his will is his love in action. And finally he repudiates the innermost reality of his own being, his vocation as a son of God. The breach caused by sin thus damages the inward man and, by shattering the concord of his being, converts the danger inherent in his concrete condition into a rebellion. In fact, the secret of man's hierarchical and progressive unity lay in communication between his soul and God, in "recollection" in the most literal sense, that is the spiritual concentration and inner presence to one's self which enables us to be in communion with Him "who is closer to us than our inmost self". Once this "recollection" is destroyed by the revolt of his will, man is driven to exteriorize himself and allows himself to be monopolized by the lower and superficial elements of his complex nature. Henceforward man's animality pursues a quasi-independent course, and sin, carrying within itself its own punishment, must now "yield increase only to death" (Rom. 7. 5), and death indicates and consummates our fall into disunion. As a result man is no longer unified and at peace with himself. The soul, no longer in a state of complete submission to its God, can no longer be completely master of the body. It no longer has the power to ennoble the body by spiritualizing it, and with the loosening of the links between the two it is the body which is in danger of dragging the soul down towards animality. Here is the primary source of the misery we experience and which leads us to echo the words of Pascal: "What a monster is man!"

But this discord, the deep-seated result of sin, is not only the straining of the relations between the two constituent elements of man's structure, the body and the soul; it is also, and on a deeper level, the soul's struggle with itself, a struggle within the same person of two "egos", the carnal and the spiritual. The real conflict is between the carnal and the spiritual man. This warfare, which is beyond our comprehension or often, rather, beyond our awareness, is for the believer more real than any mundane battles or reverses. "I stand between the angel of light and the angel of darkness," said

Bernanos, "and I look upon them in turn, with the same raging hunger for the absolute." The whole of human life is centred on this conflict, and we know the powerful attraction exerted on us by the carnal appetites, and how exposed we are to the storms that rend us asunder. Any man who experiences this conflict in his innermost soul cannot fail to echo the words of St Paul: "Inwardly, I applaud God's disposition, but I observe another disposition in my lower self, which raises war against the disposition of my conscience, and so I am handed over as a captive to that disposition towards sin which my lower self contains. Pitiable creature that I am, who is to set me free from a nature thus doomed to death?" (Rom. 7. 22–4). Through sin, the spiritual element in man appears to suffer total defeat. In any case the vital forces of personality are affected. Its inwardness bears a wound and will be less "open". Response, welcome and offering will no longer converge upon their true end, the deep-seated purpose of personality, but will fall back upon natural ends which will not satisfy them because these ends are divorced from their relation to the absolute. Man, thwarted of any effective approach to God, loses all sense of his true being and goal, and, finding himself incapable of surrendering to disinterested love, succumbs to the egotistical love of self. Sin, by disrupting man's spiritual unity, stops his movement towards God who calls him and is the end for which he is made. Herein is to be found the true Fall of Man: for ultimately man's fall is from above, since he has broken with God; the sin is first and foremost to be separated from God.[1] We can now understand how the deeper our sense of God, the more able are we to grasp the reality of sin, so true is it that the greater the saint the

[1] We know that, through original sin, man has become incapable of performing supernatural acts, and consequently of achieving salvation unaided. See, for example, Canon 5 of the Council of Carthage, A.D. 418: Man has become incapable of carrying out the divine commandments; or canons 6 and 7 of the Council of Orange, A.D. 529: Man is incapable of loving and acting supernaturally, and therefore of attaining eternal life. Nevertheless, it is interesting to note that man retains the power of accepting or rejecting God, and can still perform unaided acts which are not sins. See Council of Trent, Session VI, chaps. 1–4, canons 4–8.

greater the suffering caused by sin. When theologians speak of
the grievous sin that separates, they are referring to mortal sin.
This term, now common in Christian parlance and which has
perhaps lost something of its force, contains a profound truth.
It means that man is dead, not indeed in the physical sense, but
in the sense that the blow has been struck at his deepest and
most fundamental value, his relation to God.

It follows that because a person is a unity open to others and
to the world, this breach involves two others inseparable from
it. Man is cut off from others, from other human beings and
from the world, a fact which reveals the origin of his anguish
and anxiety in the face of his fellow men and the universe.

All sin, and consequently all separation from God, shatters
the unity of mankind: sin has social repercussions. This is profoundly true of original sin which, by ruining God's image in
man, destroyed the principle of man's communion with man,
and wounds us because as human persons we are linked with
the whole race and particularly to its head. But all sins, even
the most secret, strike at all men through the sinner, for we are
members of one and the same body. It is for this reason that
Origen declared that sin necessarily substitutes multiplicity and
diversity for unity in fellowship. Sin, in fact, by attacking a
man's inwardness, necessarily attacks his capacity for "openness" and fellowship: it destroys the principle of co-existence
in which supernatural charity consists. It is at this point that the
danger of treating our fellow men not as persons but as objects
may become an appalling reality, which appears in every kind
of oppression from torture to the reduction of human beings to
the status of tools and means to an end. A state of conflict and
struggle follows inevitably on the loss of personal inwardness,
for the person transcends both individualism and collectivism,
only when it is in diametrical opposition to both of them. It is
precisely these two terms, individualism and collectivism,
which seem to us the most distressing manifestation of man's
separation from man, springing from his separation from God.
On the one hand individualism desires to comprehend the

"ego" as an isolated and absolute entity, on the other hand collectivism holds that man is the aggregate of social relations, and defines him as a part subordinate to an absolute whole. But in the long run both individualism and collectivism derange and destroy man by ignoring the fact that the movements of expansion and interiorization are the two inseparable pulses of personal life. Sin, which is the loss of charity as between men, because it is initially the loss of man's loving relation to God, certainly seems to drive us into one or the other of these aberrations which alienate man from himself and his fellows. "Narcissus," says E. Mounier, "was devoured from within by the sickness of self-love, he melted away to nothing as he looked at himself. But Hercules was devoured from without by his final victory, and burnt to ashes by the trophy of his earthly triumph."

Finally, sin impairs man's relation to the universe. In his downfall man involved the universe, which, from being a gift of the divine bounty, became a hindrance to mankind. In the beginning man and the universe were at one. With the entry of sin they became, like body and soul, ill assorted elements. This dissociation is apparent in the Genesis story. "Through thy act, the ground is under a curse. All the days of thy life thou shalt win food from it with toil; thorns and thistles it shall yield thee, this ground from which thou dost win thy food. Still thou shalt earn thy bread with the sweat of thy brow, until thou goest back into the ground from which thou wast taken" (Gen. 3. 17–19). Our consideration of the body's nobility, as forming a unity with the soul, led us to maintain that the spirit was in contact with the universe, and could make the spirit present in it through the medium of the body. We then perceived that the deeper the unity of body and soul, the greater its mastery over the world: in other words, man's capacity to understand and control the lower forms of nature increases in proportion to his spiritual growth. This is what St Thomas means by saying that all things are in some manner contained in man, who therefore masters them in so far as he masters himself. Here we have an

elementary psychological law: the less man is present to himself, the less capable is he of penetrating and organizing reality,
and the greater his subjection to its influence. No doubt this is
only an approximation to the truth, but it enables us to understand the relation between the state of man and the state of the
universe. Once the union of body and soul, in respect of its
supernatural reality, has been strained by original sin, the bond
between man and the universe is *ipso facto* loosened. Because
of original sin, the world becomes for man an impenetrable
reality, hostile and full of ambushes, of which he can only
partially take possession after a prolonged struggle. Human sin
has sealed creation with the seal of corruption and slavery:
"Created nature has been condemned to frustration; not for
some deliberate fault of its own, but for the sake of him who so
condemned it" (Rom. 8. 20).[2]

It is apparent from the above that we can go beyond sin's
disastrous effects on man's relations with his fellows and with
the universe and discover its very root. It is the rejection of God,
a rejection which injures the most vital reality in human personality, its living relation with the Absolute. Once this fact
has been grasped as the source of the experiences we have of
our frailty and weakness, three attitudes may arise in man's
consciousness and determine the meaning for him of life, death
and destiny. They are despair, *natural* hope and *supernatural*
hope. Here we can do little more than mention them.

Despair and natural hope mark the limits to which the rejection of God can go, implied as this rejection is in the assertion
of man's absolute value and his independence. Here we touch
the very heart of modern atheism, which derives from its
denial of God the assertion of the sovereignty of man, who thus
comes to be regarded for man as the Supreme Being. But from
the moment man claims to be an absolute, and renounces any
relation or reference to a being other than himself, transcend-

---

[2] In his Christmas Allocution of 1956, Pius XII said: "Original sin and
its consequences have deprived man, not of his lordship over the earth, but
of his security in the exercise of that lordship."

ing him and making him what he is, he is bound to give way to despair or to indulge in hope. Yet both these attitudes are equally calamitous for man, and are unable to account for the concrete drama which appals any man who is conscious of and experiences his situation and status in the world. Despair is the logical outcome of a philosophy of the absurd which admits no reason for man's existence; natural hope directs man along a purely temporal line with no reference at all to the eternal. In this case man's natural hope is surely vain, since time, if it is to be real, is the sum total of a movement from positions to counter-positions ever seeking some higher position, which in its turn will have to give way to one still higher. A hope whose end is unattainable cannot be called hope. Moreover a purely temporal existence is always in danger of ending in an idolatry whose object is an abstraction which becomes supreme, such as class or race.

Because sin, by wounding the unity of man, of mankind and of the universe, is basically a rejection of God, it would appear that if man wishes to recover the dynamic movement of his whole being, his purity and his peace, he must once again enjoy a vital union with God. We have now to consider whether he is still capable of doing so.

CHAPTER V

"OUR PEACE AND OUR RECONCILIATION"

"The love of God has been poured out in our hearts by the Holy Spirit, whom we have received" (Romans 5.5).

Man, wounded by sin, retains his being as a creature invited by God to share his love, but he can no longer answer the call of his own being; created in God's image, he can no longer enter into this dialogue with Charity, "because he does not love, and is as a dead man before God". Here is the source of all his sufferings. He seems to be waiting for a new creation, but as far as he himself is concerned he waits in vain for there is no new creation apart from the grace of God. At this point God's plan is revealed as a long preparation for the Deliverer, the new Adam, the Giver of life. "The law was our tutor, bringing us to Christ, to find in faith our justification" (Gal. 3. 24). This liberating act is a new creation, a proof of the sublimity of God's love, for it is not a thing that God gives us—in any case, when God calls, his call is always the gift of his love—he gives himself so that we may have life, so that once again we may be in a living relationship with him. "What has revealed the love of God, where we are concerned, is that he has sent his only-begotten Son into the world, so that we might have life through him. That love resides, not in our showing any love for God, put in his showing love for us first, when he sent out his Son to be an atonement for our sins . . . he gave us his love first" (1 John 4. 9, 10, 19).

The whole of Christian thought concerning man turns upon this fact. God entered history in order to save man and make him a partaker of the divine life. God willed, for his own glory, that man should be fully and finally himself.

"CHRIST IS MAN"

It is not our purpose to set out the main theses of the dogma of the Incarnation, but simply to call attention to the light thrown on the mystery of man by the infinite "phenomenon" of the Incarnation, and thus to gain an insight into the concrete dimensions of personality.

Christ, the Son of God, is a man, and indeed "the complete man". All who despair of man, because he is no longer at one with the Absolute but engaged in a vain pursuit of a temporal absolute, can find peace only in the answer which illumined Pascal's night: "Not only do we know God only through Jesus Christ, we know ourselves only through him. We know life and death only through Jesus Christ." This truth offers no mere consolation to soothe away our sufferings by causing us to forget this earth, but a life-giving reality capable, by saving what is noblest in man, of restoring meaning to existence and of providing a radical justification for it.

"The Word was made flesh . . . " (John 1. 14). "His nature is, from the first, divine, and yet he did not see, in the rank of Godhead, a prize to be coveted; he dispossessed himself, and took the nature of a slave, fashioned in the likeness of men, and presenting himself to us in human form" (Philipp. 2. 6–7). These texts make it clear that his human Incarnation is the unique union of the divine nature with human matter in the one person of the Word. There is more here than a mere encounter or a mere casual contact: the Word assumes humanity so fully that he makes it his own together with all its qualities and acts. In bringing salvation to men he submits to the laws of human nature: in the words of St Paul, he is born of a woman, born under the Law. Our Lord lived and knew the processes by which a man's personal history unfolds itself in space and time. He lived the life of a Jew, he experienced the same afflictions as other men and, like them, died in the same cruel agony after he had suffered all that a man could suffer. He was a man, "surely the son of Joseph the carpenter", but we are also told that "this man was certainly the Son of God". We must grasp this unity in order to see clearly what the love of God is and to throw light on the drama of human life. He who possesses a human nature has at the same time a name above all other names. In his body dwells the fullness of divinity. St John, who was an eyewitness, could declare: "We had sight of his glory, glory such as belongs to the Father's only-begotten Son, full of grace and truth" (John 1. 14). The incarnate Word is indeed the sacrament of God in the deepest and fullest sense. He is the manifestation of God in a human nature, and the image of the invisible God. And that is why he is the sign of man redeemed and saved.

When we say that Christ is man we do not after all mean that the humanity of Christ is an ideal which man should approach by imitating it in the least clumsy fashion he can muster. Christ's presence is in human nature and in man and his presence is most intimate and most efficacious, because it is a transcendent presence.

Mankind, wounded and strained by sin, is reinstated in Christ. The Incarnation expresses man's basic relation to God: man had lost his unity by turning away from God, the Word becoming flesh weds God to humanity once again in a far more splendid way. The union of the divine and of the created is made real in Christ to the highest degree. We are therefore better able to see how daring is the Liturgy when it makes us sing of Adam's sin: "*Felix culpa!* O happy transgression, which earned for us so great a redeemer." The dignity of man is thus re-established in splendour since the vanquisher of Satan was born of the family of him whom Satan had vanquished. It is through the Incarnation that this dignity is revealed, for Christ has taken our human nature and incorporated it in himself.

Through the sufferings of the Son of God the original harmony that was destroyed is restored and enriched. True, human nature bears a wound, yet at the same time it is redeemed: though sin has darkened it and weighted it down God's grace has filled it with a greater and more spiritual light than the original creation could have made it possible to foresee. Christ is "our peace and our reconciliation" because by one and the same process his love establishes the unity of man with himself and the unity of man with man.

The appeal addressed to our first parents, and through them to all mankind, while based on their likeness to their creator, appears in a new light and admits us to the profoundest secret of the mystery of man and to the most vital principle of his unity, namely his sonship in Christ. It is his own sonship that Christ imparts to us through his humanity imbued with his quickening spirit which is his divine nature, because, as St Paul emphasizes, it is in Christ's death that we are baptized and in his resurrection that we are raised from the dead. Thus he penetrates to the depths of our being, the inner source of our thoughts and desires: "I am alive; or rather, not I; it is Christ that lives in me" (Gal. 2. 20). By his incarnation, death and resurrection, Christ makes us sons of God, that is he completes our nature through this relation to the Father, just as the Son is eternally completed in his absolute relation to his Father.

But the grace of his incarnation restores not only the unity of our individual lives but also the unity of all men with one another, for personal and communal unity go hand in hand, and the inner unity of the self, if it is genuine, must always be at the source of the spirit of universality however wide its scope.

"He is our bond of peace; he has made the two nations one, breaking down the wall that was a barrier between us, the enmity that was between us" (Eph. 2. 14). The mystery of Christ is therefore in reality the mystery of the "new Man", of that unique Body in which all men are united so that they may have access to the Father, and of which the more each individual is a living and personal member the more he labours to achieve that unity. By this means "we all realize our common unity through faith in the Son of God, and fuller knowledge of him. So we shall reach perfect manhood, that maturity which is proportioned to the completed growth of Christ" (Eph. 4. 13). By this means also this one unique living new Man, will advance under the guidance of the Holy Spirit until the unity of all mankind is finally consecrated and all men made perfect in the one God.

The incarnate Christ is therefore revealed as the "key" to the mystery of our existence in the sphere of personality, whose distinguishing mark is unity. God has intervened in a more excellent way than at the time of the creation. By assuming into himself the risk involved in creation, he, as we might say, "explains" it. His overflowing bounty triumphs over the evil inevitably involved. Through the victory achieved by his divine life in our carnal, temporal and mortal nature he transforms our fallen state into a means of salvation: in the words of St Irenaeus "the Word became flesh, he became what we are so that he might make us what he himself is". The Incarnation, by bringing man into a relation of sonship with God, centres him once more upon the Absolute, and in this sense restores man's harmonious relations with God, his fellow men and the world. "By revealing the Father and by being revealed by him, Christ fully reveals man to himself. By taking possession of man, by laying hold of him and piercing to the depths of his being, Christ compels him to go down also into himself and to discover there, as in a flash, regions whose existence he had never hitherto suspected. Through Christ Personality becomes adult and fully conscious of itself."[1] Christ, because he is Man, is truly the key to all knowledge of, and every truth concerning, man.

UNITY REGAINED AND SOUGHT

The most profound characteristic of human personality our reflexion has revealed is unity, the unstable unity of a creature

[1] H. de Lubac, *Catholicism*, p. 176.

bound to the two worlds of flesh and spirit, but a progressive unity affecting its spiritual and historical reality, and in its being created for the eternal but immersed in time. The experience we have of our condition and situation in the concrete has proved to us that in our groping efforts and our sufferings, and in this struggle between flesh and spirit, we were striving for unity. Finally we have seen that sin, the root from which all the contradictions of our existence spring, is fundamentally and of its nature a kind of wound inflicted on the unity of our being, that is in its relations with God, our fellow men and the universe. All these considerations taken together justify us in saying that as individual men in the concrete, we long for unity and we cry out for that peace which is communion. It is at this point that Christ comes to bring about this unity of our whole being in its secret depths, in a more excellent way than we could ever have hoped.

In Christ, man ceases to be merely an "image of God", by virtue of having been created by God, and becomes a "divinized" being, sharing by grace in all the depths of God's love. The double gift of existence and of the supernatural gift of life in Christ enable man's being to find its complete fulfilment in a new creation. For every move on the part of God's love there is a corresponding and new deepening not merely of man's action but first and foremost of his being, of man himself. In this living relation to Christ, we are shown the whole man and the uniqueness of his personal being; the absolute value of each individual man in his vocation as a son of God, which gives his being its unity; the brotherhood of all mankind. Thus is man fulfilled in a unity which consists of his presence to himself and his presence to others. To reveal the unity recovered by redeemed mankind is to reveal the concrete situation of the human person in his filial relationship to God and his fraternal relationship to his fellow men and to the universe.

"Seeing that we were dead in our sins, God restored us to life in Christ, so that in him we might be a new creation, a new work of his hands" (St Leo, Christmas Sermon). The term "new creation" marks the culmination of human personality in the concrete and its fulfilment in Christ. We have already pointed out that the human person in its very structure and because it is created in the image of God, is a living relationship with God, is a call to communion and fellowship with him. But the sin of Adam involved the whole human race in a severance between creation and adoption. Though we are still created in God's image, our vocation to union with God has no real power, and in the absence of a living relation to God we are unable to realize and fulfil our true nature. This is the state of the human person linked as he is with the whole human race and particularly with its head, our first father, whose fall involved our fall. Now it is precisely this living relation to the old Adam that is abolished by the redemption, which replaces it by the living relation to Christ, the new Adam, who has come to restore to man his living relation with God through his own grace as the Son. Henceforward the human person, redeemed by the Son, acquires a likeness to the sonship that is the Word's by nature. And so man's being at its root is not merely a likeness and a vocation but also a filiation, a relationship which includes the two others, and makes man "a new creature", since henceforward he is called "in Christ" and so when, sustained by grace, he answers this call, he regains his "deiform" being.

This filial relationship to God—and here we touch its depths and its repercussions throughout our whole being—is to be of one form with the Word, the unique image of God, "the first birth which precedes every act of creation . . . in him all created things took their being. . . . They were all created through him and in him; he takes precedency of all, and in him all subsist" (Col. 1. 14–18). Here we have, not a fusion, but a genuine communication, a contact between two persons in which the most intimate and spiritual unity is achieved: "It is no longer I that am living, but Christ in me." In this communion the spiritual unity of the human person reaches its maximum fullness for, since it is bound by a living link in Christ to God, it shares by a relation of sonship in the very life of God. In other words it is established more firmly than ever in its own reality and existence, it is more personal than ever since henceforth existence invades it on all sides through the soul, now truly the child of God. It is the person whose spiritual nature is transformed by this living relationship to God, in the Son: which explains why it is essential and absolutely true to speak of a new creation. Not only the being but the action of the person is profoundly affected, together with the act of the spirit which we have characterized as response, welcome and offering, an upsurge of personal being in its freedom, intellect and will.

Man, when restored by redemption to this filial relationship with God, responds by a life which brings the vital powers of his soul into play and so will draw him into the vital movement of the love of God. "To the extent to which we welcome the love of God in us, the essential tendency of this charity which has now become ours, its vital movement will be to reply to the divine condescension by a gift which is as like as possible to God's own gift. God gives to man his Christ, not only the incarnate Word but the crucified Saviour, and this is the perfect expression of his love."

The response of the person to the call of God through his Son consists in an act of faith which, by pledging the whole personality, sets the whole personality free. To show what this liberation of the personality by faith really is, we shall first state briefly what faith itself really is. Faith is a supernatural gift, not only because it sets us in the order of salvation and admits us to the realm of the love of God itself, but also because when God calls us he always gives himself by making it possible for us to hear him. God vivifies and raises us up from within, and this grace implies an answer on our part, a free adhesion of our whole soul, since we are called to enter the realm of love. This shows us that faith is in fact a dialogue between man and God, for God is the source and object of faith; this is why there is in it a form of invocation which is a summons to prayer. Faith therefore does not mean we are in contact with some remote abstraction; the term of the relationship of faith is God as he is in himself and what he has done for man. The object of faith, that is, is the mystery of God and his redeeming Love: "We have learned to recognize the love God has in our regard, and to make it our belief" (1 John 4. 16). In faith the person discovers his centre of gravity because he has come into line with the purposes of God.

Since it commits man's whole being, and is a living out of the filial relation to God in Christ, faith enables the human person to understand itself, and by transcending them, sanctifies its deepest aspirations. It is the principle of spiritual unity, and consequently of the spirit's own inwardness to itself, for by welcoming the author of its being, the human person is re-united to itself at the deepest inner level and recognizes that at the centre of its being, it is the child of God, and so absolutely invulnerable in its relations with others. We know that self-inwardness is the source of self-mastery for the human person since it directs it towards its goal. Now, for a person faith is the presence of the power of God, a power which guarantees that the spirit within it will master the flesh. "What God asks of you is that you should sanctify yourselves, and keep clear of fornication. Each of you must learn to control his own body, as something holy and held in honour, not yielding to the promptings of passion, as the heathen do in their ignorance of God" (1 Thess. 4. 3–6). Faith spiritualizes our bodies by making them the temple of the Holy Spirit. It is true that we shall always experience the dangers, the obtuseness and the sluggishness of our bodies, their sorrow, suffering and weariness, but we know that by offering them to our Lord we are converting them into instruments not of harm but of holiness. "You must not make your bodily powers over to sin, to be the instruments of harm; make yourselves over to God, as men who have been dead and come to life again; make your bodily powers over to God, to be the instruments of right-doing" (Rom. 6. 13).

By leading man to the mystery of his unity and inwardness, his living presence to God, faith affects his spiritual activity, for living faith is at the same time light and love. It is a light in the sense that it influences the intellect; not that the intellect is capable of explaining to itself, by means of clear and distinct ideas, the mystery of God, who, though drawing near to us in faith remains unique and absolute in his transcendence, but because faith is not a light that we can see, but a light which enables us to see reality through the eyes of God.

The intellect is then in a position to discover the true meaning of things. In the context of the Creator's loving plan, it can see the meaning and the profound purpose of its own life, and so attune itself to the divine vision, in the light of which it is able to test all the feelings of which it becomes conscious and all the events that occur in its life. It is therefore understandable that to the redeemed nothing is trivial or insignificant: the true charity of the redeemed, as we can imagine, does not confine itself to phenomena, but treats every man as a son of God.

Finally, faith affects the person's will and completes its liberating work by bringing the source of all love and of all self-sacrifice, God who "bows the stiff neck and warms the cold heart of our egoism," to dwell in our souls: "The love of God has been poured out in our hearts by the Holy Spirit" (Rom. 5. 5). Faith, which is allegiance to the God of love and to his plans for mankind, by guaranteeing our inwardness guarantees also our "openness": in faith we recover, but now at a deeper level than our unaided strength could attain, what we have previously called "the dynamic force" of personality, namely that process by which the more inward the person becomes, the more "open" it proves, and the greater is its capacity for welcoming others and giving itself.

If we accept the life of faith in a filial relation to God, through his Son, we shall at length receive the consecration of our personality raised up by God's grace, when we are brought face to face with him in eternity. Far from making man less a man, as claimed in the Marxist view of religion as alienating man from himself, this life in God, through and in Christ, is a fulfilment of human personality beyond the expectations of man's original creation.

Since the redeemed human person is a filial relation with God in Christ, it is also a fraternal relation with mankind and with the universe.

The act of creation called all men in Adam to unity, since all were called and created in the image of God, which was the same in each of them. Therefore sin, as a betrayal of the divine image, at the same time disrupted the unity of mankind by destroying its spiritual union. In the words of Origen: "Discord follows in the steps of sin." The purpose of the incarnation of Christ, who is the head of the human race, is to re-establish that unity, and by breaking down the barriers of hate to convert mankind into that mysterious "new man", calling men to form one single "perfect Man" in a communion of saints. This call which comes to broaden at the same time as it achieves the relationship to mankind which is a constituent of human personality, may be said to be an ontological necessity, in the sense that it is a necessary element in the being of all who stand in a filial relation to God in Christ. The redeemed person becomes a follower of Christ and an "heir of God", that is he enters into the filial relation to God which makes him truly man, only by becoming a living member of the Mystical Body and by incorporation into a new people in which there is "no more Jew or Gentile, no more slave and freeman", but which is "the Israel of God". When the redeemed man corresponds with the grace of sonship he becomes engrafted onto that great spiritual body the Church. Through the Church Life and Truth come to him and in her is brought about the most intimate union between persons, since it is a unity in Charity in which persons may hold communion in the depths of their being. Thus we realize that the call of God, which gives concrete expression to the structure of the person as a spirit, has not merely one purpose, the inward growth of the person called—this would involve the betrayal of inwardness itself— but by leading the person into his own depths, it leads him to all other men. Hence our further realization of the extent to which this relation to God fulfils personality in its spiritual being. We know, to be sure, that every call affects the inward man: as St Augustine puts it, "heart speaks to heart". But this call is always a call to share in the building up of God's people, so true is it that a soul who has received and accepted the Word of God is bound to spread it abroad since love of its nature tends to go out to others and give itself to them. Remembering the numerous calls recorded in the Bible, the call to Abraham, to Moses, the prophets, the Blessed Virgin and St Paul, we see that although this call is eminently personal, it is always concerned with a mission, with the building of the "House of God".

After incorporation into the Mystical Body through which it receives life, the redeemed person is released by the power of Charity uniting all the members from the solitude to which it was condemned by sin. Still more, its being is strengthened; in the gift received it finds itself, and its inner self is both deepened and enlarged. Persons who live by this life will witness in the world of men of which they are a part to the reality of the most profound inner life and of an all-embracing fellowship.

We are now in a position to understand that our view of human nature does not involve choosing between an enclosed inner life and a universalism emptied of inwardness: man in fact comprises within himself both these inseparable dimensions.

From his filial relation to God is derived man's fraternal relation to the universe and to his fellow men. The links which united the universe through man to God were broken by sin but restored by the incarnation of the Son of God; for "all things were created by him and for him", and in the unique Image of the Father the whole universe becomes once more an image of God and like a brother for him who shares God's outgoing love. Henceforth redeemed man recovers, in the grace of the Son, his former place in the midst of creation; he can therefore rule over it and bring it to fulfilment by leading it back to its creator. "Nature in its turn will be set free from the tyranny of corruption, to share in the glorious freedom of God's sons"

(Rom. 8. 21). The more man lives the life of a son of God, the more will he bring creation to share in his glory and the better able will he be to give back to it its true purpose—to glorify God. In the redeemed, this fraternal relation to the universe is a life of contemplation or prayer, and of work which is a form of fulfilment. Contemplation, roused by the impact of the outside world, is the fruit of a vision induced by faith: man then sees in the harmony of the universe and its rich abundance, a sign of God's majesty. At a deeper level, contemplation sees in the universe "the supreme gift of God's charity to man's charity, the supreme thanksgiving offered by the love of man to the love of God."[2] Contemplation fulfils the human person, and is possible only when a man willingly opens his heart to welcome the universe as a brother, and it springs from the gift of faith, which alone can make us see creation and its mystery as a sign of God. Then from the heart of man, obedient to God and a brother to all things, there rises the song of St Francis, who hears the inner voice of the universe and makes it rise to God. By contemplation man completes both the universe and himself, imprinting by his labour the mark of the spirit on the world, and so fulfils it and makes all that is in it sing. In the words of Claudel: "It falls to us in a masterly and methodic way to take up again all the work of Adam in the earthly paradise. And what an earthly paradise it will be when no single fragment of creation is excluded from it! It is for us to bring order everywhere, a sense of proportion, fruitfulness and law." The world was entrusted to man so that his labour might convert it into a manifestation of his spirit, the image of the divine Spirit.

Man is redeemed in Christ, and we have just seen how deeply we are affected by this redemption. Unity is recovered, but it is still a unity we have to seek. Man is redeemed but he is still on the march. He is present to the world but present as a traveller and a stranger. He has to work in time. This fact, as we have

[2] M. Zundel, *The Splendour of the Liturgy*, London and New York, Sheed and Ward, 1938.

said, is at the origin of man's history, but his goal is eternity. The final characteristic of redeemed man is that he is a pilgrim of eternity in time. Thus we are able to grasp the direction of our journey and the meaning of our condition.

Man's life in Christ is a life begun but not yet stabilized; it must lead to the full adoption of the sons of God. Our salvation is in the present, but also in the future.

We are crucified to a world in which we nevertheless have to live. Human life, like all created things, consists of darkness and light. "All things human have their dark aspect, to which alone they owe their living, fleshly reality. Light is enhanced, not diminished by darkness." As we face our pilgrimage, as it really is, our first attitude—and it is rooted in our faith—should be to accept this paradoxical reality, this state of tension. We shall always be in danger of denying this tension, for we realize that it constitutes a risk. But all is over for the man who seeks satisfaction in forgetting. He will in fact be no longer "open" to God who can ground him in Charity. The state of tension, and the dialectic of our pilgrim's progress are rooted in the duality of our being which is both of the flesh and of the spirit. Our redemption by Christ and our reliance on his Word entail our cooperating freely in the redemptive process and day by day our life must be lived more and more through our filial relation to God in Christ and our fraternal relation to our fellow men and the universe.

There are three characteristic features of the tension experienced by the pilgrim of eternity in time: advance, struggle and history.

Redeemed man is a developing being, he is moving towards a unity which becomes increasingly profound. We know that the human person, since he is incarnate, is in danger of allowing himself to be submerged in the material world, and is consequently bound to affirm more and more often the presence of the spirit. Life, in all its spheres, and at a deeper level in that of the spirit, is a reality on the march, spiritual realities can only be living realities if they progress, failing which man is confined to a world of objects to be possessed, whereas his true destiny is to exist spiritually and so to advance through all vicissitudes in response to the call of God. Spiritual realities are on the march, they are dynamic, not static.

St Augustine observed that man must always seek in the expectation of finding, and find in the expectation of continued search. This is the very law governing our adoption as sons of God: "You are to be perfect, as your heavenly Father is perfect." The spiritual life of man consists not in having a fixed ideal, which he may approach more or less successfully, but in entering more deeply into the mystery of the divine love, which cannot be grasped by any unaided human effort.

Human existence, since it is progress through tension, is a struggle characterized by the fact that it is not the acceptance or repression of either of the terms in the tension between body and spirit, time and eternity, but the deeper understanding and acceptance of both. It is true that through redemption man shares ontologically in the death of Christ, but spiritually he must make this death efficacious day by day (1 Cor. 9. 24); the struggle is between the carnal and the spiritual man, the prize is life in Charity through the spirit. The meaning of this struggle imposed on the redeemed in their pilgrimage may be defined as a choice. It is by choosing God that we achieve spiritual unity, and the choice means that we have daily to call upon God: we cannot play a double game, we cannot be both temporal and spiritual, we cannot cling to the earth and its allurements as well as to God and the treasures that are his. It is therefore evident that the choice which is the crux of the struggle involves our tearing ourselves away from all that threatens to close us in upon ourselves or to bind us to the world of objects. The Cross now appears upon the horizon as the sign *par excellence* of this struggle between sin and love, death and life.

The tension characteristic of man's earthly existence is history, or more accurately history in the making. Man becomes a historical being through his body, which subjects him to the conditions of space and time. But his true history is the progress of his whole being which he brings to fulfilment at the price of struggle. In other words, the history of redeemed man is a pursuit of self-unity, which is the perfection through grace given and accepted of the threefold relationship which makes him a man; and this perfection in the process of becoming, as it is, consists in the insertion of eternity into time. Therefore it is clear that redeemed man lovingly accepts these temporal and "fleshly" realities, since it is through and by them that his history unfolds itself at his instigation, and he himself goes forward towards that culminating point of this history, the moment of transfiguration.

THE ACHIEVEMENT OF UNITY

All life begins and ends in an act of sacrifice. The life of man redeemed began by the sacrifice of God's Love: "When a man is in Christ Jesus, there has been a new creation" (Gal. 6.15); and this sacrifice bears fruit in the individual man in the gift of faith and free submission to the mystery of divine love. This life has continued through the vicissitudes of time and along the pilgrim's way. It has been accompanied by acts of sacrifice to which the pilgrim committed himself increasingly day by day. Finally life culminates in a sacrifice which will integrate our gift with the total gift of God's Son. We lose ourselves in death to find ourselves as God wants us to be in the eternity of glory.

DEATH

Because he is involved in time and history, and, at a far deeper level, because he is a sinner, man is exposed in his existence to death, which becomes for him a daily possibility. Is death an abrupt end to man's slow and painful advance towards unity, or does it come to set a sacred seal upon it? Does it prove the absurdity of human life and the futility of all our endeavours, or does it impart a meaning to our existence by being not an end but a resurrection?

These questions become present to our awareness even in the

midst of activities that are of the most vital concern for us and in which we offer ourselves up not to death but to life. We feel that in death, the central question "What is man?" in which all other questions issue and meet, finds its ultimate foundation, for death is the final challenge to man. After the death of a dear friend, St Augustine says, "I became a riddle to myself, and I asked my soul why she was sad and gave me such disquiet, but she did not know how to answer me." We know from experience that this challenge can arouse in us a feeling of the mystery of life, since it obliges us to face the mystery of our existence and of our relation to being. It follows that to put questions to ourselves regarding death is neither an idle pastime for the mind nor an indulgence in morbid introspection. It is a specifically human activity, a sign of genuine manhood, for man by losing himself seeks to find himself, and to throw the whole weight of his personality into transcending time without denying its reality.

This problem, as we noted in our analysis of anxiety, lies at the heart and centre of every man, for the instability of his existence is brought home to him by the set-backs and disappointments of life, the possible betrayal of the love he hoped would last for ever, the process of growing old, and the loss of his loved ones who, since "we die alone", seem to cease all communication with him, and abandon him to solitude. What is the point of life if it inevitably ends in death, if at every turn it progresses "by kind permission" of death? No doubt we can look on the death of others as an inescapable commonplace of everyday occurrence, or as the fulfilment of a fate which we are bound to accept. We may drown our sorrows in amusement, or we may echo the words of the wicked in the Book of Wisdom: "So brief our time here, so full of discomfort, and death brings no remedy! . . . Whence came we, none can tell; and it will be all one hereafter whether we have lived or no. . . . Come then (they say), let us enjoy pleasure, while pleasure is ours; youth does not last, and creation is at our call" (Wisdom 2. 1–9). Nevertheless the enjoyment of pleasure does not delay the imperceptible approach of death, and when a man looks his own death in the face, there is no place for amusement or forgetting. It is "our own" death that confronts us: in the words of Rilke, "We are but the bark and the leaf, but the fruit at the heart of all things is death, that mighty death each of us bears within himself, and which finally decides what the meaning of life is." It follows that a man's attitude towards life is largely determined by his attitude towards death. What, then, we must ask, is the meaning of death?

We know by experience, since we are always in danger of shifting our being from its centre by adjusting it to matter or the flesh, that we are all constantly tempted to regard death as an absolute end, in other words we are tempted to prefer time to eternity, and so to sever our basic relationship with God.

This temptation has become a reality (but in the form of an inquiry into man's existence) in contemporary philosophy of the "Existentialist" variety, particularly as propounded by Heidegger and Sartre. According to Heidegger we are essentially creatures born to die. Our life doubtless moves inexorably towards death, but above all life is for each of us his most personal and most genuine opportunity and yet, at the same time, the opportunity is itself an absurdity. So to live, genuinely to live, is to be constantly expecting death, possibly imminent death, which puts a final end to our existence. Sartre, reacting against this conception of death as the ultimate possibility in man's existence, concludes that death is a negation of man's possibilities and therefore beyond his control: it is purely a fact, radically contingent and absurd, which we cannot grasp, which comes to us by mere chance and from without. Both birth and death are inexplicable surds. Nevertheless, for both Heidegger and Sartre death comes to crown the radical absurdity of our existence. Such is the strictly logical conclusion of a philosophy of immanence, and a philosophy of the absurd and of despair, for which the living are already "dead but unburied". This is inevitable in a doctrine which systematically and from the outset posits anguish, the experience of our radical absurdity, as the sole criterion and the sole means of reaching genuine existence. Starting from this arbitrary assertion it is easy to represent any *a priori* thesis as a datum of experience. Moreover, with such a basis this view rejects as unauthentic any deep-seated experience of a longing for survival after death, and yet such a longing seems to be rooted in every man's consciousness. In fact, if death is the absolute and final seal set upon life, it would appear that man's action would be destroyed at the root and become a crumbling ruin in which his freedom would be in danger of disappearing. Or again human action might well sink to a state in which all the pledges man gives are corrupted or perverted. Such an attitude towards death is correctly described as despair.

In contradistinction to this philosophy, Dialectical Materialism offers men hope. Like any other philosophy, it is aware of the problem of man in face of death, for the central point of all thought is man in his limited and contingent condition. It has been justly defined both as a "humanism of struggle", since man, a product of matter, becomes himself through his struggle with nature and society, and as an "eschatological humanism", because it holds that the ultimate goal is not society but the collective man of the city of the future where all strife will have been replaced by universal peace, and man will be master of his fate, untrammelled by the conditions which at present render insoluble all specifically human problems. From this point of view Marxism proposes to direct man's deep-seated longing for survival by genuinely offering him the hope of a future mankind in which all that is human will be found in all its fullness. Death is still a problem only because the times we live in are inhuman: men die, but they will survive in a humanity they will have created by their labour, and their death will be its very life.

We now have to ask ourselves whether at the level of the personal subject this theory does not go counter to man's basic demand to understand, here and now, the ultimate meaning of the trials which beset him. Even if he dies for the sake of the mankind that is to come, will not his death always be his own, with all it implies in the way of heartbreak and tragedy which he alone can experience? This question can be answered in the negative only on the basis of a refusal to regard man as essentially a being with an inner life of his own.

Furthermore, since man, as we said in regard to personality, is a historical being, Marxism offers itself as a purely temporal because materialistic dialectic; as such in the hope of survival through posterity that it proposes (in other words a human race which has been rediscovered by the abolition of all forms of appropriation) it seems to be driven back on an internal contradiction. In fact, if duration is the totality of the dialectical spiral of thesis and antithesis always in search of a higher level which will be transcended in its turn, Marxism is faced with these alternatives: either contradictions are to disappear so that mankind may attain total being, in which case there will be no more history since there can be no more duration; or else man kind will keep its historical character, in which case an unending dialectic will embark on a desperate course in which the present, and especially the past, will always be sacrificed to the future. In that event death will finally triumph and hope, deprived of any object, will come to an end. In other words, hope, if it is to withstand death, must aim beyond and through time at eternity. It then becomes supernatural hope, the presence of the eternal in time and for which the end of earthly history is not death, but resurrection.

In the presence of death this hope is both light and strength for the Christian. Like other men he experiences the horror, the last agony, and the physical fear inspired by the coming dissolution of his being, but unlike them he knows that Christ by his death has vanquished death. "Death is swallowed up in victory. Where then, death, is thy victory; where, death, is thy sting?" (1 Cor. 15. 54). In fact, for man redeemed, death is not a natural disaster, setting a seal on the meaningless nature of life, but an essential element in his existence, and for him it sets a seal on the original break with God: "Thou mayest eat thy fill of all the trees in the garden except the tree which brings knowledge of good and evil; if ever thou eatest of this, thy doom is death" (Gen. 2. 17). Christian man cannot escape the pains of death, but because he has been given to share in the death of Christ he will rise with Christ and live with him. To the justified sinner death is not an irreparable breach but a bridge. The justice he has received he now lives by in Christ: he is really and truly a new being, issuing forth from the eternal youth of God. Nevertheless, he is not rid of the old Adam: even though redeemed he bears the mark of sin: though redeemed he remains a wounded being. And so he must suffer death, but the drama of death, though it is still there, loses its tragic significance since supernatural hope gives him the promise of eternal life, and this hope may be so strong that it raises the soul beyond all fear and dread.

> What would it avail me to rule over the whole world? What have I to do with the kingdoms of the earth? I should be prouder to die for Jesus Christ than to reign over them all. It is Christ whom I seek, who died for all men. . . . At the moment of death I shall enter into life. . . . Have mercy upon me, brethren: do not prevent my birth into life, do not seek my death. It is to God that I wish to belong: do not deliver me over to the world and its temptations. Allow me to arrive at the pure light: it is then that I shall attain true manhood.[3]

Or again, St John of the Cross asserts that the soul which loves God looks on death as a lover and spouse, and has a greater desire for the day and the hour of death than any king on earth for his kingdoms and principalities. By sharing in the death and resurrection of Christ—and this is the basis of the Christian's belief that he himself, body and soul, will rise from the dead—redeemed man has become a son of God, and this sonship seeks its consummation in the unending colloquy of love with the Father. It is obvious that the longing to escape death rooted in the structure of the human person now drives its

[3] Letter of St Ignatius to the Romans. Ancient Christian Writers Series, Vol. I, London. Longmans, and Westminster, Md, Newman.

roots deeper still, for it is founded on the grace of man's adoption as a son of God, and on his faith in the person of the dead and risen Christ.[4]

Christianity believes in the resurrection of the whole man, body and soul, and that the soul bestows its own perfection and immortality on the body, its temporal companion. "This corruptible nature of ours must be clothed with incorruptible life, this mortal nature with immortality" (1 Cor. 15. 33). This is the Good News preached to all mankind by Christ, who rose from the dead. In the words of the Mass for the dead, *Vita mutatur, non tollitur*, our life is not taken away, it is changed. Death does not engulf all that we are; it is its gateway to resurrection.

As we saw in our inquiry into the reality of the soul, its integrity is impregnable, nor can the destruction of the body lead to that of the soul. At the same time we noted that the human soul does not of itself constitute a person since it is of its nature to be united to a body which is an integral part of the human person. Accordingly the soul, when parted by death from the body, its helper in time, must experience a feeling of deprivation. At this point philosophy raises the question of the possibility that the soul's desire for reunion with the body may one day be realized. It is not impossible, and that is as far as philosophy as such can go; we must leave the realm of mind and enter that of charity; we then find in revelation the complete answer to man's longing for physical and spiritual immortality. The point we wish to make here, after explaining in the previous paragraph what death means for the Christian, is the remarkable way in which the grace of God fulfils completely and out of pure love man's longing for the unity of his whole being in eternity.

Because he is endowed with a soul, man has access to a

[4] This explains why the Church insists that the Son of God really died. She does so in particular as against Docetism, a generic word used to describe the error of those who refuse to admit that Christ was man. The Church's insistence on this truth dates from the earliest days of Christianity; see, for instance, the Epistle to the Colossians.

transcendent world. He is a being with a spiritual vocation and destined for a life in God. As we have seen, this is the profound purpose of human personality. But his forward movement seems to be thwarted, it is as if sin had attacked him at the point of junction between his body and his soul. Consequently his desire for survival remains a force operating, so to speak, *in vacuo*, and, as in Marxism, is in danger of finally becoming a monstrous desire to transform time into eternity. Since grace perfects nature, only our burial with Christ in his death can explain why our whole being longs to survive. For the Christian faces death no longer as a grievous fatality but as a daily reality, since "it is in the death of Jesus Christ that we have been baptized", and it is our duty to live this grace of baptism every day. Supernatural hope, which stands at the point of intersection of time and eternity, is thus based on God's promises. Faith and baptism, by which we are "taken up into" Christ's death and resurrection, are guarantees that our longing for unity will be satisfied, and that at the end of time our body will triumph over death and will live for ever, transfigured by the immortality of the soul. "You have undergone death, and your life is hidden away now with Christ in God. Christ is your life, and when he is made manifest, you too will be made manifest in glory with him" (Col. 3. 3).

At the same time man is not, in his present condition, wholly imbued with grace; his spirit is not completely master of his body. As we have said, one of the most exact descriptions of Christian man is that he is a pilgrim. It is true that, by the grace of baptism, he has risen with Christ, body and soul; but this resurrection is not yet made wholly manifest. "We ourselves, although we have already begun to reap our spiritual harvest groan in our hearts, waiting for that adoption which is the ransoming of our bodies from their slavery. It must be so, since our salvation is founded upon the hope of something" (Rom. 8. 23). Therefore, in practice, the concrete problem for man is to make his death subserve his life. This he can do only by and with Christ, by the arduous pursuit of the unity of his whole being, body and soul. And this being is both of time and of

eternity; it is through time that he is in contact with eternity
His inspiration is in the Beatitudes, the song of supernatural
hope on the lips of those who are journeying towards eternal
life. Christian man knows that his inner life will reach its fullness only in the life to come.

Because man is a unity that exists by the subsistence of the
spiritual soul communicated to the human composite, the
whole man longs for immortality. Nor does he hope in vain,
because Christ came to save the whole man, transforming by
his death the mystery of the destruction of the body into the
mystery of its restoration to life. "This corruptible nature of
ours must be clothed with incorruptible life, this mortal nature
with immortality. Then, when this mortal nature wears its
immortality, the saying of Scripture will come true, Death is
swallowed up in victory" (1 Cor. 15. 53). Then will the gates of
the kingdom be opened.

ETERNAL LIFE

The whole of the history of man and of humanity is a progress towards the one and perfect heavenly Jerusalem and to
its nuptials with the Lamb. Death is the way through which we
go to it. The heavenly Jerusalem is the city of God, for "the
glory of God shines there and the Lamb gives it light". It is the
city of unity, for when "all things have been made subject to
him . . . then the Son himself will become subject to the power
which made all things his subjects, so that God may be all in
all" (1 Cor. 15. 27). It is also the city of the fulfilment of the
"new man" who has attained his perfect stature, it is the city of
the eternal present. The human mind is slow to grasp the true
nature of eternity because for us the essential thing often is to
live intensely in time, and we forget that our presence in time
derives all its value from the presence within us of the eternal,
we forget that our life is only a history because it is a response
to the eternal in the concrete circumstances of the journey of
our existence. These simple observations make it possible for us

to realize that eternity, already present in our life in time since it gives that life a meaning, cannot in any way be the abrupt and inexorable cessation of our existence in history, since it is by our conduct and life in time that we shall be judged. Eternity is therefore rather the transfiguration of our existence; and so, as we have said, the term of earthly history is not death but resurrection, bringing life not to an end but to fulfilment. Hence, we should not imagine eternity either as an indefinite prolongation of time or as time at a standstill, for such an eternity would freeze life, and would be neither its resurrection nor its fulfilment. Nor is eternity a kind of duration, very different no doubt, yet merely following on that of the world in which we now live. We might tentatively describe eternity as the absolute Act, as total perfection; in other words as God himself, the presence of God in an "eternal today", the very inner being of God, beyond the realm of becoming, for he is the eternal Living Being. To enter the kingdom, therefore, is, for us, to be in God, to live by his life, to enter into Christ's glory as the Son of God (all these terms indicate an intense life). "This, Father, is my desire, that all those whom thou hast entrusted to me may be with me where I am, so as *to see* my glory, thy gift made to me, in that love which thou didst bestow upon me before the foundation of the world" (John 17. 24). And in his First Epistle the Apostle adds: "But we know that when he comes we shall be like him; we shall see him, then, as he is." This vision of the inmost life of God—and the vision *is* life with God—is eternity, which can therefore be expressed only in terms of life, not in terms of space and time. Eternity being the transfiguration of man, then appears as the fulfilment of man in his twofold relationship of son of God and brother of all men. It is the achievement of humanity's destiny and of the unity of mankind, it is the wish uttered in Christ's prayer "that they may all be one; that they may be one in us, as thou, Father, art in me, and I in thee" (John 17. 21). It is the deep purpose inherent in the human person, the final goal towards which all men strive.

Hence eternal bliss excludes any illusory utopia in which all contradictions would have disappeared. It is the life of God himself and so is the foundation of the pilgrim's supernatural hope.

Eternal life may be understood on the analogy, constantly employed in Christian tradition, of a city. "Jerusalem, the divine city, the promise of blissful peace. Blessed above all brides, thy dowry is the glory of the Father. Heavenly city, thou owest thy splendour to thy union with Christ the King." St Augustine calls it a "radiant dwelling-place". In this city of God the deepest inner life and the most vital universalism come to their fruition for it is a city built of "living stones"; a city of brothers, a city of sons.

It is a city of sons, because man face to face with God will attain through Christ to the fullness of his being as a son of God, a being for whom there is neither shadow nor change. In this living and eternal relationship with the Father, man will achieve his unity, since he will be in communion with him who gives him being, who is the source of his existence, the centre of his love. His unity will be a unity of the whole man, of body and soul, for the mortal body will become immortal, and instead of being an impediment and a burden will become simply a means of expression and communication. But at the same time eternal life is a city of brothers, built on the pattern of the communion of the three divine Persons in the Trinity, into which all the just will be gathered, in which, says Origen, all the members of Christ will be knit together, each in its own place, and the whole multitude will form one body. Brotherhood, whose establishment is man's noblest purpose, has a precarious existence in this world; the world to come will set an absolute seal upon it.

Thus does eternity transfigure man in all the dimensions of his personality, his unity, inwardness and "openness", his inner reality which gives him being as the image of God, his relationship of a son to the Father. And so "the blessed can see themselves in their own depths because they possess the light, not of the sun and moon, but the very glory of God. And the blessed can see into the depths of all the elect for they shine with the same light and are as luminous to others as a jewel of crystalline jasper. The love that flows from them is spread abroad in these others who in their turn enter into them by the outpouring of their own charity.[5]

This heavenly city is brought into being in the resurrection of Christ, yet it still has to be established and built, for mankind is only on the road to unity. It does not guarantee the Christian a pleasant escape from the toil and suffering of human life, but offers him supernatural hope, thereby acquiring for each one of us an absolute value by admitting us to citizenship while we are still living in the world of time. This life eternal for the Christian, whom it will transfigure and perfect, is not a world beyond, for in supernatural hope it is already here. For him it is a living and present reality. The Christian knows that it is by implanting eternity in time that he advances towards eternal life, thus bringing his own history and the world's to their fulfilment. The Christian citizen of the city of "the flesh" is already a citizen of the Kingdom of God, but he knows that he will become a worthier citizen if he impregnates this world with the presence of God. The heavenly Jerusalem is a gift of God, but man, living with God's own life, labours to build it, uplifted by the hope that eternal life will crown his earthly pilgrimage.

5 J. Huby, *Mystiques Paulinienne et Johannique*, pp. 222–3.

CONCLUSION:

TOWARDS UNITY

Our study of the Christian view of man has been governed by one major concept, that of unity. We have met it at each stage of our journey, or rather it has run like a thread throughout the discussion. Were it not for the futility of attempting a single all-embracing answer to the question "What is man?" we might say that he is a unity in search of itself, in the making and ultimately achieved, and that, through all the pleasures and pains, the meetings and partings which form the rhythm of his earthly pilgrimage, and even through the breach caused by death, he remains essentially a seeker after unity. Unity is probably the most genuine mark of man. It expresses his inmost being both as a spirit and a body, in the existence with which he is invested by the spirit, and at the same time reveals the ultimate meaning of his quest and of his progress in response, welcome and self-sacrifice. It is undeniable that man has to become himself, and that he can do so only by achieving the unity of his whole being, which is also a union with mankind and the realities of time. It is for each one of us a fact of everyday experience that a man who loses or is robbed of his natural unity soon becomes a mere plaything for himself, or an undifferentiated part of a whole, and the consequence of loss of unity is ultimately death. Unity, we may say, is the centre of gravity of human existence, it is through unity that man finds himself and men find one another, and by this double discovery, come to see the meaning of existence. Therefore acceptance of unity is acceptance of the human realities as they exist in man's being and in his journey through time. This fact invites us to recapitulate, in the form of a synthesis, the essential characteristics of man's unity, and from this point of vantage to see how his "acceptance" is brought into play. To be brief, we merely insist that man's unity is both structural and functional.

Structurally, man is the union of body and soul in the unity of the existence with which he is invested by his spirit. We indicate this first characteristic of man's structural unity when we say he is a "person", in whom the greatest fullness of existence is found and enables him to exist within himself and to be "open" to his fellow men. A new characteristic then comes to light; it is the second aspect of this structural unity. The human person in his unity is a centre of relationships. Basically he stands to God in the threefold relationship of likeness, vocation and sonship. He is related to men as a member of the world of men and entirely within it, and to the universe because situated through his body in space and time, to which moreover the presence of his spirit gives a meaning. Finally, and this is this unity's third characteristic, by the very nature of his structure, which is flesh and spirit, we have seen that the human person is an unstable and incomplete unity who has to become himself at the cost of effort.

This real unity, although ambiguous and unstable and all the more so because it is that of a being wounded by sin, requires the individual man to accept himself, that is to recognize the reality of his being for what it is, and it is both darkness and light, strength and weakness, shallows and depths, flesh and spirit. The first step in self-acceptance is to recognize these limitations, since to do so opens the way to an authentic existence for man who thus rejects none of the elements of which it is constituted. Such a rejection, which is equivalent to death, springs from the refusal to admit the existence of shadows or limitations, and so the fact that all that is human is both of the flesh and the spirit is ignored, as also the fact that in man the shadows, far from destroying the light, enhance it. If man rejects his complex unity he makes himself unable to live as a man, and is in grave danger of lapsing into angelism or animality, neither of which is human in any sense.

When we say that the unity of man is incomplete and unstable, we are asserting its character as a "functional unity", achieved by the progress of the human person bringing his vital forces into play, his freedom, intellect and will, in the strictly spiritual acts of response, acceptance and self-sacrifice. These acts exemplify the essential law of the human person's authentic existence. This law is that the greater his own inwardness, the greater his capacity to become universal, that is to welcome others; and the more he welcomes others in his capacity as a spirit, the more he enters into his own depths. But this functional unity, because it is the progress of an incarnate person, is a unity of strife and tension which becomes, owing to sin, a struggle between the carnal and the spiritual man. It is then that acceptance develops from recognition into response to the deepest inherent purpose of the human person, and the human person is a capacity for fulfilment and transcendence if and when God's call is answered. This response, since it is that of an incarnate freedom, is correctly termed a choice. Hence we may say that it is our choice of God which brings unity to our hearts, guarantees the stability of our existence and a meaning in our progress. We could not remain at this level without losing our grasp of the concrete condition of the human person, wounded yet redeemed. So Christ was revealed as the very centre of our unity: in short, to answer the call of God is to enter into the mystery of Christ, the mystery of the "New Man". For this reason acceptance was transfigured into an act of faith; a gift of God who in giving himself makes it possible for us to hear him—and this grace implies a response freely made with all our being. Once the human person has entered by faith into the mystery of God and of his redeeming love, he exists in a unity which is a filial union with God and a brotherly union with his fellow men and with the universe, a unity which, while making him share our Lord's Cross, brings him along the way towards the perfect unity of eternal life.

Man is this living unity. This, we believe, is the witness Christian anthropology can bear in man's favour, and this the light it can offer man's consciousness as he asks himself this eminently personal question: "I am a man, but what is man?" This is why a Christian anthropology is, in the last analysis, an urgent summons to exist, that is to achieve this unity. It is at this point that such an anthropology will have its greatest impact on the contemporary world, which in its quest for unity seems to swing either towards the denial of unity when it declares that life is absurd with death as its absolute end, or towards the out-and-out affirmation of unity conceived essentially as social unity. At the present time the function of Christian thought concerning man is surely to demonstrate that unity, in all its dimensions, is the very principle of authentic existence.

SELECT BIBLIOGRAPHY

BIVORT DE LA SAUDÉE, Jacques de (Editor): *God, Man and the Universe*, London, Burns Oates, and New York, Kenedy, 1954.

CARREL, Alexis: *Man the Unknown*, London, Hamish Hamilton, and New York, Harper, 1935.

COLEBURT, R.: *An Introduction to Western Philosophy*, New York, 1957, and London, 1958, Sheed and Ward.

HAWKINS, D. J. B.: *Man and Morals*, London and New York, Sheed and Ward, 1960.

LUBAC, H. de, S.J.: *Catholicism, A Study of Dogma in relation to the Corporate Destiny of Mankind*, London, Burns Oates, 1950, and New York, Longmans, 1951.

MARCEL, G.: *The Mystery of Being*, London, Harvill Press, 1950, and Chicago, Regnery, 1951; *Metaphysical Journal*, London, Rockliff, 1952; *Being and Having*, London, Dacre Press, 1948

MARITAIN, J.: *The Person and the Common Good*, London, Bles and New York, Scribner, 1952.

MOUNIER, Emmanuel: *Be Not Afraid*, London, Rockliff, 1951, and New York, Harper, 1954; *Character of Man*, New York, Harper, 1957.

MOUROUX, J.: *Meaning of Man*, London and New York, Sheed and Ward, 1950.

PASCAL, Blaise: *Pensées* (Everyman edn, 874), London, Dent, and New York, Dutton, 1951.

TEILHARD DE CHARDIN, P.: *The Phenomenon of Man*, London, Collins, and New York, Harper, 1959.

TRETHOWAN, Dom Illtyd: *An Essay in Christian Philosophy*, London, Longmans, 1954.

The Twentieth Century Encyclopedia of Catholicism

The number of each volume indicates its place in the over-all series and not the order of publication.

All titles are subject to change.